THE
LAST LOVE
LETTER

An ex-armed forces officer, **Kulpreet Yadav** is the author of seven books, two e-books, and one collection of short stories.

Shortlisted for prestigious writing awards and winner of the prize 'Best Fiction Writer, 2018' at the Gurgaon Literature Festival, Kulpreet lives in Delhi.

THE
LAST LOVE
LETTER

Kulpreet Yadav

RUPA

Published by
Rupa Publications India Pvt. Ltd 2019
7/16, Ansari Road, Daryaganj
New Delhi 110002

Sales centres:
Allahabad Bengaluru Chennai
Hyderabad Jaipur Kathmandu
Kolkata Mumbai

ISBN: 978-93-5333-507-6

First impression 2019

10 9 8 7 6 5 4 3 2 1

The moral right of the author has been asserted.

Printed at Nutech Print Services, New Delhi

For Leah.
Your spontaneous creativity and quick wit
turns our days beautiful.

Chapter 1

My dearest Akash,

By the time you read this letter, I will be gone. Remember when you wrote your first love letter to me? You said that letters have permanence. I want us to be permanent, even though I want you to forget me.

I'm writing this letter in full command of my senses. I want you to know that. The disease is killing me slowly, but it has yet to reach my brain. I know that, soon, I'll be in a lot of pain, and I also know that you will be there by my side through it all, with our beautiful creation, our daughter, Sara. I can't promise not to cry out in pain and subject you to sleepless nights as you run between our home, your office and this hospital, but I'll fight as best I can. Like a candle in a storm, I'll burn my brightest, thinking about you, about us, and about Sara.

I've led a happy life, Akash. Back in college, when I met you for the first time, I knew you were the one for me. Your eyes spoke to me even before you did. But we didn't get off to a great start, did we? We argued over silly things related to the college festival, and I thought to myself, this man is so different in his head, his heart and his eyes, all at the same time. The next day, when you walked towards me in the canteen—I'm reliving that moment as I write this, and it's giving me goosebumps—I knew what you would say. You said you wanted to discuss it once more. And when we did, we agreed on everything, a few issues my way and a few yours. I felt comfortable with you from that moment on. In many ways, you completed me. I found calmness. We met numerous times after that. One day, I wrote this in my dairy: *You can't keep falling in love with the same person over and over again unless his smile and respect for you are real.*

I love your smile. But more than that, I fell in love with you because you respected me. Did you know that from that day in the canteen till this very moment, I never stopped telling myself how lucky I am? You, Akash, are the best thing that could have happened to me. And now we have our Sara.

The pain is back, and since I know that you are expected in the hospital at any moment and I don't want you to see this letter yet, I must hurry up. I've asked my nurse, Angel, to give this letter to you after I'm gone. She will visit our home and hand this to you one month after I'm dead and cremated. Gosh, I feel so frightened even thinking about death. But all of us have to go sometime, I know, so it's okay. Please give one pair of my gold bangles to Angel. She likes gold, and I've realized that she has a heart of gold too.

You're only thirty, Akash. Please, before you read further, close your eyes and promise that you will agree with what I'm about to say.

Come on, close your eyes now.

Sooner or later, someone will get close to you again. Please allow it to happen. Don't ruin your life thinking about me. When you find someone, I want you to fall in love again. Think of that woman as me, and you can be happy again. I want you to be happy, I want Sara to have a family, and I want to be forgotten. I want you to merge us with your new life and start again.

Those who are lucky to be in love live a thousand years because in each moment, they live a thousand moments. I've lived a thousand years with you, Akash. Thank you for being such a wonderful lover, a great father and an amazing friend. I hope to meet you again, somewhere among the stars. I know our eyes will find one another, no matter how large the galaxy might be.

Don't curse the disease, don't let thoughts of me make you unhappy; instead, think of all the beautiful moments we have shared.

Give my love to Ma and tell her that I love her very much.

With all my love for you and Sara,

Your lucky wife,

Nisha

Akash rubbed his eyes and turned to look at Sara. It had been one year since Nisha left the two of them alone. He wiped away the tears and smiled at the picture of Nisha that stared back at him from the wall above the bed.

'I miss you, Nisha.'

It was almost midnight, and the day at his office had drained him completely. But like every day, he could not sleep without reading Nisha's letter. It had become a ritual. He wanted his last thought before sleep to be of Nisha. He caressed Sara's hair and stared in amazement when she smiled in her sleep. Sara had Nisha's eyes and hair, and many times when he met her eyes while saying something, he wondered if it was Nisha looking at him through their daughter's eyes.

The nurse, Angel, had visited one morning a month after his world had been devastated. He was all alone in his first-floor apartment in Greater Kailash in New Delhi. Sara was away at her grandmother's house in neighbouring Gurgaon. He didn't recognize Angel instantly, but when she introduced herself, he remembered her from the hospital.

'Sir, Nisha Madam left this letter for you.' She extended a folded piece of paper towards him.

He plucked it out of her hands, started to say something but failed, and finally sat on the sofa to read it. Yes, it was her. He recognized the handwriting in a flash. He looked up. 'When did she write this?'

'Sir, on 3 January, one week before she passed away. That morning, she was feeling a lot better, and both of us knew that it was only a matter of time before…'

'I know. Please, can I read this alone?'

Angel nodded and left as Akash started to read. He read the letter several dozen times that day, and when night fell, he continued to reread it until pain and exhaustion sent him to sleep, the letter still caught between his fingers.

After two days, he visited the hospital and presented the bangles to Angel. He'd had them gift-wrapped, with a label that read, 'For dear Angel, from Nisha.'

'Sorry, sir, I can't take this.'

Akash showed her the letter, and after some persuasion, she agreed to keep them.

'You know, sir, your wife was the kindest person I've ever met. Good people always die young. I'm so sorry.'

Chapter 2

'Dad, I don't like sandwiches in tiffin every day.' Sara looked up innocently, a drop of milk hanging from her chin and the bowl of Chocos unfinished in front of her. The school bus was expected in ten minutes, and Akash had packed a cheese and tomato sandwich for her school snack.

He looked at her, exasperated. Before speaking, he smiled with as much sincerity as he could muster. 'Beta, every day I make you a different sandwich. Come on now, hurry up. Finish your breakfast or you'll miss the bus.'

Sara made a face and went back to eating. Akash grabbed her shoes and helped her put them on as soon as she had finished. Then he wiped her face, picked up her bag and extended his finger, all in one motion. Sara grabbed the finger, and they left in a hurry.

When Akash got back home from the bus stop, he had just thirty minutes to prepare for work. He moved from one room to the next, realizing the apartment required serious cleaning. He did have a maidservant to clean up, who picked up the keys from the landlord's ground-floor apartment an hour after he left, but she had been away that past month, and Akash hadn't been successful in finding a replacement. Akash did a bit of tidying up and decided to leave the proper cleaning for Sunday.

Everything in the apartment reminded him of Nisha. This was the home she'd come to as a bride five years ago, and they had visited the various markets together to buy crockery and furnishings. Though both knew that it was a temporary arrangement and they would eventually buy their own place when they could afford it, they had spent most of their savings on making the apartment look like the home they had dreamt about when they were dating. Just one year after their wedding, they had brought their little Sara to this very apartment. It was here that she had learnt to crawl, take her first steps and form her initial words.

Akash shaved quickly, not actively noticing but still aware that ignoring his health and working overtime in office had dulled his personality. The clear black eyes no longer belonged to the person who had been madly in love with his wife. His face was missing the radiance that only happiness could bring. His 5-foot-10-inch frame seemed less commanding due to lack of exercise, and his once-boyish, crew-cut hair was now long and messy.

Akash got under a hot shower, vaguely aware that his distraction would delay him and that he should hurry up and focus on work instead. He stood under the sharp spray with his eyes closed, the hot water falling on his back, his senses adrift and his mind filled with memories of Nisha.

Have you ever noticed that we keep our eyes closed in the shower but always keep them open in the rain?

He was taken back to the time they had got drenched one July evening while shopping at Sarojini Nagar. Nisha had pulled him to the park close by, and they had stood in the rain for a long time, holding hands, not talking, just breathing—peaceful, soaked and with their eyes open—before Nisha had whispered that.

Akash got out of the shower, dressed in a suit and tie, and looked at the clock. Just like every day, there was no time left for breakfast, and he was soon in his car, on his way to the office in Connaught Place on that cold February morning.

Chapter 3

'Akash, we need a new strategy to impress our client. The last two proposals you made were rejected. This is our final chance. We can't afford to lose this contract.'

Raichand Kapadia, his boss, spoke slowly, deliberately, barely audible. Fifty years old, Raichand had been running Prime Focus Advertising Agency for the last twenty years. He had hired Akash when Akash was in his final year of college. Short and plump, Raichand was a quiet man with a reputation for being a great observer of life, and a closet poet, who was witty and smart. Today, however, he seemed dishevelled. His hair seemed a little out of place and his tie was way too loose.

'Sir, I have been working on a new concept. It should be ready in a week, tops.'

Raichand was on his feet. 'A week? They want it by tomorrow, Akash. I reminded you two days ago, didn't I?'

'Yes, sir. I'm sorry, sir.'

Raichand sat down again and pointed to the chair on the other side of his large desk. Akash, who had been standing so far, sat down too. 'Listen, Akash, I'm sorry for your loss, but it's been a year. You should recover faster. Nisha would have wanted you to do better at your job, don't you think?'

Akash looked up, nodded, and left the room. The mention

of his wife's name had made him uncomfortable. *What has she got to do with it?*

Akash got back to his desk and plunged into action. When he looked up a few hours later, he realized that he should have left for home an hour ago. He picked up his keys and ran to his car.

Sara was in the ground-floor apartment of the landlord, where, at that time of the day, their domestic help, an old man, was the only person present. Akash could tell that she had cried, but by the time he saw her, she had stopped crying and was looking out of the window. The old man stared at her from his chair not far away.

Akash knew the old man was a harmless octogenarian who had lost his ability to speak due to old age, which had also impaired his vision. The landlord—a cheerful Sardar named Lakhwinder Singh, or Lucky, as everyone, including Akash, called him—said that the old man had been with them for the past sixty years, and though he was too old to work, he was allowed to stay, as he had no family of his own. Forty-year-old Lucky, who lived alone because he had lost his mother and father in a plane crash, was the old man's only family.

When he picked Sara up and thanked the old man, Sara didn't hug him back. It took the entire afternoon—telling her stories, talking to her and making her faces—to make her look at him as she usually did. Finally, around 8, when they were watching a cartoon show together on television, she laughed, and he knew everything was okay again. He'd been successful in turning her around this time, but what if it happened again?

He ran their daily routine in his mind. His boss allowed him two hours off in the afternoon so he had enough time to get back home, be present when Sara arrived by bus, prepare her lunch and put her to bed for an afternoon nap before heading back to office. In the evening, Akash got home just after 5 every day, but to compensate, he worked the missed hours from home.

'Now, what do you want to eat, Sara?'

She looked up briefly, declared 'pizza and ice cream' with a smile, and went back to watching the cartoon.

That evening, Akash ordered Sara's favourite pizza and stepped out of the apartment to visit the shop at the end of the street to buy her favourite ice cream as soon as they'd finished the pizza.

An hour later, when she was tucked in bed, well fed and deep in sleep, Akash looked at the picture of Nisha that hung over the bed and smiled in relief. Then he took out the letter and read it a few times before losing himself to sleep too, his palm resting on Sara's hair.

When Akash woke up, it wasn't on account of his alarm clock. It was due to fear. He flung the blanket to one side, switched the lights on and peered at the wall clock. It was 4 in the morning. He switched his laptop on and, as it was booting, walked across the hall to the kitchen and prepared himself some black coffee.

The coffee calmed him down a bit and he started to work. It took him three hours to gather his notes and ideas, and give them a final shape, just in time to wake Sara up for school.

His mother was away at an ashram in Haridwar, and he missed her support at this crucial time. But he knew that his mother had had it very rough these last ten years due to his father's ill health. His father had passed away two years ago, and she still needed to stabilize herself. He couldn't think of burdening his mother with his own problems. Sara had been his and Nisha's responsibility, and now that Nisha was gone, she was his responsibility.

When Raichand studied his plan later that morning in office, he smiled and said, 'I think this will work. I still feel it lacks something, but I know you've worked very hard on it, so let's give it a shot.'

'Thank you, sir.'

That afternoon, the clients visited the office, and Akash was encouraged by the way they reacted to his presentation. But when they called an hour after leaving, they'd decided not to use it.

'It's a good strategy, Mr Akash, but after some thought, we think it won't work for us at the moment. It lacks vitality. We're sorry.'

Prime Focus Advertising Agency lost a major client that day, someone who had been with them for ten years and was one of their main sources of revenue.

His boss left office without a word to anyone, and Akash wondered what to do next, his eyes on the clock as the time approached for him to leave for home and be with Sara.

Chapter 4

There is no rock bottom in love.

Subah had believed in this idea completely. It wasn't a quote from a famous person but something that Subah, a painter, had scribbled in her dairy in one of her contemplative moments when she had still been in college.

But she'd been proven wrong. Reality was different from her expectations, and the man she had loved and trusted with her life turned out to be a cheater.

She had faced him, saying, 'Together is forever, you said...'

He had looked up, his arms still around the woman Subah hadn't known existed until that moment, and said, 'Did I? Let me rephrase that—together is just a moment.'

She'd raised her hand to hit him but had left the room in a rage instead, screaming.

Subah's rock-bottom moment had happened when she was in love. It was an irony that she couldn't come to terms with, so she'd decided to tear that page from her diary and throw it away forever.

It had been three years since that day. Subah was twenty-five now and had never again allowed a man to get close to her. There were many who'd tried, and some had persisted for months, but she had ignored them all. Her life was dedicated to painting and running her NGO, Help Forever, through which she helped broken women put their lives back together. She helped spread awareness, raise money for specific causes and arrange free vocational training at leading institutions for the deserving women. She helped them reclaim their lives and stay away from men. In all, she had helped more than a hundred women, and her efforts had been praised by the Delhi government and many other corporations and media companies.

'Subah, coffee.'

'Thank you, Bala.'

Subah put her paintbrush and palette away, pushed aside a lock of hair that had fallen over her face with the back of her hand, and collapsed into a cane chair. She looked at the unfinished painting. She had not given it a name yet.

On the canvas was what looked like a puddle on the road, in which was reflected the image of a woman who held a rose in one hand and a baby in the other. The painting was in different shades of grey, except for the eyes of the woman, which were bright red. The woman's eyes spoke the language of the fire that was raging in Subah's heart. But the painting was a work in progress.

She picked up the coffee—a well-deserved break from working all morning. Her studio was in a barsati on the roof of her two-bedroom DDA apartment in Vasant Kunj, where she lived alone. Her father was in the United States, employed by an IT firm in a senior position, and her mother was with him. Subah saw her parents twice a year. Once when they travelled to India, and the second when she visited them in the US. She loved spending time with her mother, but had never liked her father. He was another reason for her immense dislike of men.

Years ago, after her college graduation, when a few of her friends were hanging out, not prepared to say their goodbyes yet, she had confessed her feelings to a close friend.

In fact, it was her friend who had initiated the topic. 'I love my dad and mom—they're so understanding. Guess I'm very lucky. You never speak about your dad, Subah. Why?'

'Well...I think it is because I *only* like my mom.'

'And your father?'

'Let's talk about something else, okay?'

Subah was so frightened of her dad that she kept her feelings about him to herself. Her frustration about the ill treatment her mother received was kept locked in the innermost part of her heart. In fact, she had not mentioned what she thought of her father to anyone, not even her mother.

On the other hand, her greatest worry was that slowly, without wanting to, she would turn into her mother. In time, she, too, would have a husband, someone who would turn her into an inanimate object, an accessory to be used only when required and neglected when not.

'Why? Are you afraid of your father?' her friend persisted.

'Look...' Subah thought for a while, and then something snapped in her head. 'I hate my father, okay? And I'll always hate him. He...he is a typical, old-fashioned Indian man. Do you know he's never been there for my mother? She raised me and my brother entirely on her own. He always comes home late at night, drunk and foul-mouthed. And he doesn't respect my mother one bit. Forget about respecting her, he doesn't even acknowledge her presence. The lady of the house is not allowed to make a single decision related to the family, however small. I've seen my mother spend her entire life either waiting for him to return home or mustering the courage to seek approval for a matter related to the family. All his life, my father has taken my mother for granted, using her for housework and making her feel insecure and insignificant. As a kid, I saw this neglect and lack of love break my mother, even though she never complained.'

As soon as Subah finished, her palm flew to her mouth and covered it.

Why did I say all this?

What will happen now?

Due to her loud monologue, a few of her classmates had gathered around and were staring at her. Their expressions were unreadable. Did they feel sorry for her or did they think her complaints were unjustified?

Then, after a few seconds of pin-drop silence, her friend clapped and the others joined in.

'Subah, the first step is to communicate. Because only when you communicate can your innermost feelings, your fear, be diluted. I feel sorry for your mom. But something tells me that you won't be like your mom.'

'Perhaps…' She looked at each of them, and that was all she could muster the courage to say. After that day, whenever she met her friends, no one brought the topic up.

Subah's brother, Rohan, had died in a traffic accident when he was just eighteen. Though her mother never mentioned it, Subah thought visiting India reminded her of Rohan. She seemed more at peace in the US.

Chapter 5

*I*t was a glorious sunny afternoon, the temperature around 15°C, when Subah finished her lunch, changed into a polo-neck sweater and jeans, and went out in sneakers, making her way to a nearby park. With high cheekbones and shoulder-length hair ending in wild curls that bounced as she moved, Subah was 5-foot-4, neither petite nor too tall. But because she was slim, she seemed taller than most women her height.

To counteract the intensity of the mood she was trying to create in her painting, she needed fresh air and all the brightness that a winter day in Delhi could offer. She had completed one round of the park when her phone rang.

'Hello, is this Miss Subah?'

'Yes?'

'I'm calling from the India Habitat Centre, New Delhi. You applied to hold an exhibition from 1–31 March. I'm calling to let you know that the dates have been finalized and you should make your payment within a week.'

'Thank you.'

It was Subah's tenth exhibition, and the second at the Habitat Centre. She had gotten the dates she had wanted, but her work was far from ready. She decided to return home immediately, gathering her thoughts about the work to be done. She had less than a month before the exhibition began.

As she passed a garbage bin on her way back, she thought she heard the sound of a baby crying. She looked around but couldn't see anyone. She heard the crying again and stood on tiptoe to peer into the bin. And there it was—an infant resting on a pile of rubbish, everything but its head covered in a white towel.

She picked up the baby, which felt terrifyingly small and fragile in her hands. Was it a boy or a girl? How old was it? A day old? A week old? A month old, perhaps? She had no way of knowing. She looked around to see if she could spot the mother, but saw no one. Who would leave an infant in a garbage bin?

The baby had stopped crying. When she looked down, it had opened its eyes. Was that a smile? Their eyes met, and the baby blinked.

'Poor thing, where's your mother?' she whispered.

Subah decided to wait. Soon, there would be a lot of people around her. She held the infant closer when she sensed movement in her hands. Her maternal instincts had taken over. Was the baby cold? Hungry? Uncomfortable?

She felt the tiny face move against her skin and stop after a few seconds. The baby was quiet now. She pulled it closer and felt for a moment that they had become one. The new and the not-so-new creations of God.

For the briefest of moments, she felt the baby's pain. If nothing was done, she knew this baby would starve to death in a few hours.

After waiting for an hour, her worst fears were realized. The baby's mother had indeed abandoned it. But why? No mother would do such a thing. It was against the laws of nature. Perhaps the mother feared for the child's life. Perhaps the child was safer here than with her.

The mother was trapped, without a doubt, with someone she considered a threat to the child's safety. Perhaps she feared nothing more than that person. Subah realized that she wasn't angry with the mother. As always, she knew, it was a *man* who was responsible for this baby's condition. The woman, always the victim, and the man, always the tormenter. Nothing had changed since the Stone Age as far as the man-woman equation was concerned.

Subah's decision was swift. She would save the child's life.

She hailed an autorickshaw and took it to the police station. The staff there was known to her because of her NGO. They swung into action, and someone from an orphanage was there in an hour to take the baby.

'Would you like to suggest a name, Miss Subah?' the woman from the orphanage asked her.

'I'm not sure...'

'We urge people who find abandoned infants to name them. It establishes a bond and encourages them to come anytime to see the child if they wish to. But it's optional. So if you don't want—'

'Khushi. That should be her name. Someone who brings joy to everyone, even though her own parents chose to abandon her.' By now, she knew the infant was a girl.

'Khushi it will be then.'

A feeling of contentment settled upon her as she heard the name.

Subah signed a few documents, and when she was done, watched Khushi and the woman from the orphanage leave.

Chapter 6

When Akash arrived at his office the next day, he saw a stranger sitting on his chair. 'Hey, good morning. This is my desk.'

The man looked up, scratched his goatee and said in a voice full of surprise, 'Sir, I've been asked to sit here. I'm new, and today is my first day.'

Akash dreaded what was about to come next even before he asked the question. 'Who hired you?'

'Mr Raichand Kapadia.'

Fear and failure swept over him, overwhelming him so much that he grasped the corner of the desk to steady himself.

The man got to his feet. 'Are you all right, sir? Can I help you to your cubicle?'

Akash raised his hand and, after a few moments, said, 'I need to take my items from the desk.'

'The drawers are empty. I'm sorry, I didn't know this was your place before. Even the cupboard over there is empty.'

'There was a picture of my wife and daughter on the desk...' Now that the man had gotten up, Akash could see that his favourite photo, which he had looked at fondly many times during the day, was also missing. 'Do you know where my stuff is? I need my things.'

'I'm sorry, sir, I have no clue. Perhaps the HR will know. Look, I'm really sorry...'

Akash didn't wait for the final sentence, and instead started to rush away from the place he had worked in for the last four years. He went past several cubicles, heard someone call his name, walked past Mr Raichand's office without looking through the glass doors and drove back home.

As soon as he got home, he opened the cupboard in his bedroom and pulled out a bottle of Scotch whisky. He opened it and drank a few mouthfuls straight from the bottle. The alcohol burnt his mouth and brought tears to his eyes. He looked up at the picture of Nisha and murmured, 'I'm sorry, Nisha. I should have worked harder. I should have been more careful.'

Akash's main worry was keeping a roof over their heads. He was still paying off the loan he had taken during Nisha's treatment at the hospital, and without a job, he would be ruined. And Sara's quarterly school fee was due next month. He drank some more and allowed the alcohol to put him to sleep in a chair in the bedroom.

The shrill sound of the doorbell woke him up, and for a few moments, he wasn't sure where he was. Was he still at the hospital, waiting for the doctors to emerge and tell him how Nisha was doing?

The doorbell rang again.

'Hello, Akash.' It was Mr Raichand. 'Can I come in?'

'Yes, sir.'

Akash led the way to the living room, where they sat on the sofas opposite each other.

The two men sat in silence for a few minutes. The last time his boss had visited their home was during Sara's second birthday. Back then, it was a noisy house, full of children and the delicious smell of food, with colourful balloons everywhere. It was quiet now.

'Akash, I'm sorry...'

'I understand, sir.'

'Here.' His boss extended an envelope towards him. 'This letter says you are on paid leave for six months and are welcome back after the leave.'

Akash looked up. He knew his boss was a kind man, but this was uncharacteristic of him, particularly when the company was struggling.

'I know about the loan. I'm your boss, Akash. Take a few months off. Look after yourself. Travel with Sara. Rebuild yourself, find your edge.' With that, Mr Raichand was on his feet.

'Thank you, sir.'

'I hope to see the original Akash again soon. Your belongings are in my custody at the office, and I'll be happy to hand them over the day you rejoin us.'

After the door closed behind Mr Raichand, Akash whispered, 'The original Akash is long dead, Mr Raichand.'

He walked back to the bedroom and took a few more gulps from the bottle. This time when the bell rang, he knew who was at the door.

'Sara.' His face lit up.

'Dad, I'm hungry.'

Akash staggered to the kitchen and looked around. He had not thought about lunch. 'Did you finish your tiffin, Sara?' he shouted from the kitchen.

'No, I told you, Dad—I don't like sandwiches.' Sara sounded annoyed.

This wasn't going very well. His daughter was hungry, and there was no way he could fix something in a hurry. Akash wasn't a good cook. He got back to the bedroom, helped Sara out of her school clothes and into what she had picked out on her own from her small cupboard, and then dashed out the door.

'Pizza again, Dad?'

'Sure. Or would you like something else today?'

'Yes, a burger and a toy.'

'Great, let's do it.'

Chapter 7

*T*he first day of the exhibition went well. After a fortnight of back-breaking work, painting almost sixteen hours a day, Subah was finally able to finish her pieces on time.

She had called her mom a week before the scheduled opening. 'It's on, and I want you to come, Mom.'

'Sorry, honey, we can't come this month. But best of luck. We're sure our darling daughter will do us proud and have a great exhibition.'

Subah knew why they wouldn't come. The anniversary of her brother's death was a week after the exhibition began.

Her father didn't call to wish her luck, not that she'd expected him to. But she knew her mother would be thinking about her constantly, and that thought gave her strength. On the first day, she had a decent turnout of media for the opening because her invitation read like this:

The exhibition Alone to the Moon and Back *will be launched by someone who is a symbol of grace and charm, someone we should admire and respect as much as we respect the best in the world of art. Be there to find out who she is and be prepared to fall in love with her.*

The exhibition was opened by Bala, her maidservant-cum-studio assistant. Bala had been rescued from a prostitution racket when she was just fourteen. She had lost her ability to speak and think, and had spent many months recuperating in a mental hospital. When she had finally recovered, Subah had brought her home.

Bala sometimes wrote poetry, and Subah had painted one of her poems on a canvas that she called *The Mirror on the Moon*.

People murmured as the sari-clad Nepali woman with the expressionless face stepped forward and cut the ribbon. The clapping, which began with hesitation, soon became loud enough to last longer than usual, its echoes hanging in the air for several seconds after people had stopped clapping. Tears slid down Bala's cheeks, but she stood motionless, her face without any expression.

The coverage in the newspapers the next day and the day after didn't match the admiration and respect the people of the media had shown at the opening. Subah had expected that and smiled as she won the argument with herself over whether people cared for those without money and influence.

Two of her paintings sold on the first day, but the second was slow, as it was a Monday and not many people visited. The lack of newspaper articles further stopped information about the exhibit from getting to the masses. In short, even though she was happy to have achieved something that she believed in, her strategy was beginning to hurt the success of her exhibition.

On the third morning, she was surprised to see a man walk in with a little girl of around five. Not many people with children visited art exhibitions, so it was a welcome change. Subah loved children and rushed to greet the little girl.

'Hello, little one, what's your name?'

'Hello, Subah.'

'Wow! How did you know my name?'

'It's written outside. Simple.'

Subah tapped the back of her head in mild admonishment and smiled. 'But what is yours?'

'Sara.'

'That's a beautiful name.'

'I know what your name means. It means "morning", right?'

'Yes, sweetheart.' After straightening up, she turned her attention to the girl's father. 'Your daughter is very sweet.'

'Thank you! My name is Akash.'

'I didn't ask your name.'

'No.' He hesitated and stammered, 'No, you didn't. I'm sorry.'

Subah turned back to the little girl, who brought a smile to her face. The girl had, by now, walked away from them towards one of the paintings, oblivious of the tension between her father and this woman.

'Dad, come here. Look, there's a snail.'

Akash headed in her direction, passing Subah and in the process accidently brushing her shoulder. She spun around. 'Mister—'

'I'm sorry, I didn't mean to.'

Sara's attention remained focused on the painting, and once again, she missed the tension.

Subah looked at the man in front of her closely. He seemed sincere in his apology. Dressed in jeans and a white linen shirt under a navy blue sweater, he seemed stressed. Was he scared of what she would do now or was he nursing some pain…or maybe ill health?

'It's okay,' she finally said, without a smile. Subah caught up with Sara and said, 'You know what? You're right, it is indeed a snail. Only smart people like you can make that out. Can you tell me where this snail is? What is that round thing?'

'Is it the moon?'

'Bingo.'

Akash walked quietly over to them after a few dazed moments and stood there without a word. Why was this woman so rude to him but so sweet to his daughter? Maybe it was the pressure of handling so many uninterested buyers, who walked in all the time. She was undoubtedly beautiful, he'd noticed, and her big, round eyes were so intense that they could penetrate anything. This woman, despite her short temper, was sure of herself. That much was certain.

An assistant appeared at Subah's side and whispered something in her ear.

It was the moment Akash was waiting for. He grabbed Sara's arm. 'Honey, we've got to go.'

'Dad, wait. I want to see all the paintings.'

'You're just a kid, sweetheart, and this is not for you.'

'No, you are a girl and you are not allowed. The themes here are anti-men, and you shouldn't see that.'

Akash turned and saw Subah staring at him. What she said made no sense. This woman not only had an attitude but was totally insane. *How could they allow such a neurotic person to hold an exhibition here?*

'Dad, I want to go now.'

The child had finally understood the tone of her voice and demonstrated which side she was on.

Akash grabbed his daughter's wrist and escorted her out without any further conversation, his ears straining to hear any final comment the crazy woman might make behind their backs.

When he reached the door, he turned to look back but couldn't identify her in the sparse crowd. 'Good riddance,' he murmured.

Later, at The All American Diner, father and daughter ate a breakfast of eggs, toast, butter and marmalade, which Sara washed down with juice while Akash preferred coffee.

'Dad, I like that painter woman. I want to become a painter too.'

'Huh?' Akash didn't say anything else. They had finished eating and were now walking back to their car.

'Dad?'

'Yes, beta?'

'I know you miss Mamma.'

He stopped, knelt down and smiled. 'You're right, honey.'

'Me too.' She hugged him with all her might.

Chapter 8

Subah felt bad about the way she had treated the complete stranger. All he'd been trying to do was introduce himself because she had spoken to his daughter. It was mere courtesy, but something had snapped inside her. Was it just because he was a man, and men were untrustworthy and capable of masking their feelings?

But he hadn't just introduced himself—he had brushed her arm too. Subah touched her bare arm now and closed her eyes, imagining the stranger's eyes on her as he approached her from behind. She shivered. And where was the creep's wife?

The Habitat Centre was not a shopping area, so she couldn't have been away shopping. He had probably left her at home and brought the daughter to make new woman friends. Or maybe he had divorced her and levelled baseless charges against her and gotten custody of the child. This man, like every other man she had met, was a cheap, opportunistic pig, whose sole aim was to use women and destroy their lives. But Subah was different— she had learnt how to survive and help those who were weak.

Her heartbreak had made her stronger, wiser and capable of dealing with all the men in the world. She had also been witness to her mother's abuse. Therefore, whatever the situation, Subah knew how best to keep men at bay.

The ringing of her phone cut through her thoughts. It was 7 in the morning, and she was about to get out of bed to get ready for her exhibition. She smiled when she saw who was on the other end of the line.

'How's it going, beta?'

'Mom, it's not going well. Out of the forty works, we've only been able to sell two so far.'

'Oh…but don't you worry. You still have many days to go. Maybe people will learn about it from the newspapers and plan a visit closer to the weekend.'

'This time the newspapers didn't cover my story, Mom. That's the problem. I think asking Bala to open the exhibit was not a good idea. They wanted a celebrity, a real celebrity with Botox and enhanced lips and breasts. Someone who could satiate their eyes and give them juicy gossip about a film star or politician. Basically, a middle-aged bitch.'

'Beta, I know you're right, but—'

'Mom, I'm sorry. I shouldn't have used those words.'

'No, but…look, it can be fixed. Why don't you find another way to let people know about the exhibition?'

'But Mom, the question is how.'

'How about advertising?'

'That costs a lot of money.'

'I'm not talking about newspapers, beta. I'm talking about social media. I know you're not fond of social media, but there are small, inexpensive companies that can make sure your ad is seen by hundreds or thousands of people for a small cost. I'll talk to your dad—he'll get home from work anytime now—and we'll find someone who can target customers from here in the US.'

'Mom, *no.*'

'But…'

'I will think about it. Thanks, Mom.'

'And please take care of your health. Don't overwork yourself. I'm sure you need money too. I'll ask Dad to transfer some into your account.'

'Mom, no, please don't. I can take care of myself.'

Subah felt a wave of anger rise inside her. She had never borrowed money from her father and never would. If anything, she wanted to help her mother become financially independent so she could decide to buy clothes when she wanted or use it for things her father wouldn't allow. That wasn't possible at the moment, she knew, because Subah was broke.

After she hung up, she thought about what her mother had said. Though she couldn't afford a newspaper or a magazine ad, she could definitely spare a few thousands on a social media campaign.

After a quick shower, and dressing in jeans and a polo-neck sweater that covered her entirely—to avoid being ogled by men at her exhibition—she looked at herself in the mirror. She knew that supposedly she was beautiful, but ever since the man she was in love with had rejected her for another woman, she hadn't been so sure. The thought made her bitter. She pulled her hair back, turned her face to see how well it complemented her tight jaw, pursed her lips and moved to the breakfast table. There was no need for make-up.

'Good morning, Subah.'

'Good morning, Bala.'

'I'm sorry, but I overheard what you said to your mother. Didn't I tell you that I'm jinxed and you should never involve me, as it can only bring you bad luck and nothing else?'

With that, she began to cry. Subah pushed back her chair, walked to where Bala was standing and wiped away her tears. Flooded with pain and regret, Bala sank to her knees, her shoulders sandwiched between the wall and Subah. Subah sat down beside her on the floor. The marble floor was cold, and a chill seeped through her jeans in just a second.

'Look at me.'

Bala raised her eyes and saw her saviour through a cloud of tears. 'I'm jinxed, Madam. The sooner you realize that, the better. It is my shadow that is ruining your show and your career.'

'No.' Subah wiped her tears away. 'And I have told you many times to call me Subah, not Madam.'

Bala didn't answer, but looked away.

'I'm not worried. I'm proud of the fact that you opened my exhibition, and something tells me it will be my most successful one yet.' Even as Subah said this, she thought about the rent to be paid and the groceries to be bought. She had no savings, and her credit card was maxed out. She placed Bala's head in her lap and sat there for a few minutes, her eyes on the wall, her morning tea long turned cold on the table.

Life is about recognizing sadness and choosing to give it a limited time, she murmured. It was something she'd once told Bala. But at that moment, sitting in the low ebb of her life, she was speaking to herself.

Chapter 9

*A*kash was seated in a café with his best friend, Rohit. The two had gone to school together, and though Rohit had gotten into medical school later and moved to Jaipur, while Akash had studied English Honours at Hindu College, they'd met regularly during vacations when Rohit came to stay with his parents at their Defence Colony house.

'I'm sorry to hear about your job, Akash.'

Akash put his cup of coffee down and said, 'You know, Rohit, I don't blame Mr Raichand. He needs someone who can keep his mind on work, unlike me, who's always thinking about home, and Sara's meals, and her homework.'

A plate of sandwiches waited on the table for them to eat, but neither seemed interested.

'It's good to know that your mother is back. That will allow you to take care of yourself. Look at you, Akash, you need to curb your drinking.'

'What? Who said anything about drinking?'

'I'm a doctor, remember?'

'No, I mean, yes, of course you are a doctor, but my drinking is under control.'

'*I am the doctor*, and that is precisely why I'm telling you this. I can see the signs.'

'Like what?' He straightened his back.

'I know from your eyes, your skin, your handshake, your walk, your posture, your...everything! And I'm your friend—don't forget that.'

'You are my best friend, Rohit. I promise to be more careful.'

'Great. So how's your mother doing?'

'Mom's good. Her trips to Haridwar usually energize her and distract her from thoughts of Dad. But it's temporary—she'll be moody and sullen in a few weeks again. At present, Sara is giving her a rough time.'

'That reminds me—why don't you take a trip to Haridwar too? I mean, I know you aren't much of a believer, but the change in scenery might help, don't you think?'

'Come on, you think I'm old enough to go to Haridwar to find peace?'

'No, I didn't mean take a trip like the old do. Just a holiday at a good resort, booze, of course, and lots of rest. Let's do it together. Sara can stay here with her grandmother. Let's do it this weekend.' Rohit laughed, pushing up the sleeves of the sweater he was wearing. The excitement in his voice matched his actions.

'It's a good idea, but, sorry, maybe some other time. What I now need is to occupy myself. I have no idea what to do with myself every day.'

'Hmm... Let me think and see if I can help you with that.'

They finished their coffee and asked the waiter to take the sandwiches away. Outside, night had fallen, and soon Rohit would have to leave for the 7 o'clock shift at his clinic. But he wanted to stay a little longer with his best friend. He called the clinic, which was just a five-minute drive from where they sat, and asked his assistant to inform him the minute someone walked in. That allowed him to stay longer, trying to brainstorm what his best friend could do now that he didn't have a regular job.

What was Akash best at? He had always been the creative kind, fond of books, ideas, poetry, etc. And his interests fit well with his job as a creative director in an ad agency. Maybe he could do something along those lines. His face brightened up as an idea began to take shape in his mind. 'Tomorrow is my day off, Akash. Let's have lunch together at Odeon Social in CP.'

'Sure.'

'One of my friends, James, he is an…err...a tech specialist... he'll join us too.'

'Great.'

They parted after a hug.

Chapter 10

The three men met at Odeon Social for lunch the next day. James turned out to be a doctor who had left his profession and become an entrepreneur. He wore an earring and had long curly hair and sad eyes. Eyes are said to be the mirror to people's souls, but that rule of thumb didn't apply to James. He was tall, happy and exuded an energy that equalled the enthusiasm of Akash and Rohit put together.

By the time they had had two beers each in their stomachs, they were feeling light and humorous about anything any of them said. There were no pretences, and it was exactly the kind of party that Akash needed. These were friends, just friends, who didn't need anything from each other except a few silly jokes, lots of laughter and bear hugs.

So when Rohit said that James wanted to tell Akash something that would help him endure the six months comfortably and also make money, the party took a turn for the serious. It was a jolt, and all of a sudden, the place started to look different. The music seemed too loud, the beer perhaps a shade bitter and the food more salty than Akash preferred.

'Listen, Akash, Rohit told me about your creative instincts and the sad thing at your office.'

Akash waved the concern away, indicating that it was all

well, and wondered what would come next as James continued: 'Look, I'm an entrepreneur, and I can help you set up a creative ad agency, a business under your name. You could serve your clients from anywhere you want, including—this is going to surprise you, but I'm not going to say your home, because that's what you would expect—your bathroom. Yes, as long as you sit on the pot with a laptop in your lap, you are in office. No more brick-and-mortar offices, my friend. That's it. What do you say?'

To Akash, it sounded like a weird plan made up at the spur of the moment. He hesitated, wondering what to say.

Rohit seized the opportunity to clear the air. 'Whoa, wait a minute, quick-gun Murugan.' Since James was from Tamil Nadu, Rohit addressed him thus for fun. 'Akash needs to understand. Let me interpret this for you, Akash.' He turned to look at his friend. 'What he is saying is he can help you set up a website, which will be your ad agency, and you can find clients and work online.'

James smiled and raised his beer. 'Exactly that.'

Akash needed time to allow the proposition to churn in his mind. He knew online companies were common now and that many did good business. He had read about such ventures in the newspapers. But could he do it? Could he be a faceless operative, sending emails to people he had never met, sharing videos, ideas and presentations online? And even if he were hired—because he could offer good rates, as there was practically no overhead—would it all be worthwhile? It seemed so dull to seal a deal, or not, while remaining faceless. 'Not a good idea, I'm afraid. I don't think I should be getting into the same business that Mr Raichand has a stake in. Moreover, I'm technically still his employee, and he is paying me. I haven't been fired and can return after six months.'

'Well, you have a point, but what are you going to do for the next six months? Just sit and drink and burn your insides? What about Sara?' Rohit's words stung hard, but Akash stayed quiet. He knew his friend was right about his increased dependence on alcohol these days. After a minute, Rohit said, 'Sorry!'

'No, I see your point.'

After lunch, when they were walking to the parking lot, Akash hugged both of them again and promised to think about what they'd discussed.

Later that evening, after Sara had gone to sleep in the other bedroom with her grandmother, he looked at the picture of Nisha and thought about his future.

The future is an illusion that takes us away from the past. But the past makes us smile, reminds us who we were, what we did. The past is real, whereas the future is just a chimera.

He and Sara did have a future, but he couldn't help looking back again and again. He tried to sleep but couldn't. Finally, around midnight, he opened the cupboard and grabbed the whisky, wandered into the kitchen to find a glass, trying his best to make as little sound as he could, and poured a large slug.

The alcohol burnt his stomach and, after the momentary discomfort, began to warm his body. He sat in the living room for over an hour, thinking about the past, the present and the future. When he finally got up to go to bed, he noticed someone else sitting on a dining room chair. That part of the living room was dark, and the surprise threw him off balance. He leapt to the light switch and turned it on. There she was, his mother— the woman who had given him life, the woman he had helped overcome the grief of her husband's passing. This woman now sat quietly, her cheeks wet with tears.

'Mom?'

'You were the one who used to say to me, "Mom, we need to overcome sadness. We need to look at those around us, those who are still in this world", and now this…' She pointed at the bottle of whisky.

'I'm sorry, Mom.'

She got up and hugged him. 'Don't be sorry, be strong. Be *you*.'

'I'm trying my best, Mom.'

'No, you aren't. Look at the future. Pull yourself together. You're not making your dead wife proud by doing this. She would want you to be happy, us to be happy, wouldn't she?'

'You're right, Mom, you're right.' He hugged her back, and they stayed like that for a few minutes. He felt like a child, happy to be protected by his mother, and no harm could come his way as long as his mother stood between them.

Chapter 11

With just one week remaining for the end of her exhibition, Subah turned to the Internet and googled companies that could help her reach more people. After an hour of searching on a day when hardly anyone came to visit her exhibition, she found a company that responded to her query in less than ten minutes. She quickly set up a meeting on that same day, timed to coincide with her lunch break, and promised herself to return as soon as she could. To deal with the payment issues, she spoke to her credit card company, and since she had never been late with a payment, they increased her credit limit by another lakh. So she had funds now, sufficient to cover the groceries, the ad expenses if she was satisfied with what this company offered, and the rent. In short, she now had ammunition to survive another month.

The agency was called Johnnie Sparks, and the man who replied to her email signed his message with that name. The meeting was set for a café in Khan Market, easy for her to reach and quickly get back.

Fifteen minutes before the scheduled time, Subah departed from her exhibition after instructing her assistant and hailed an autorickshaw. Her car was in the basement of the Habitat Centre, and since finding a parking spot at Khan Market during lunch hour was tough, the autorickshaw was the most convenient option.

She was there at 1 on the dot. But there was no sign of the person she was expected to meet. Mr Sparks was probably still on his way. She ordered coffee and a cheese sandwich.

Perhaps it was time to return to an idea she'd recently had for herself. *An hour of doing nothing except drinking coffee and thinking about life is a great investment in understanding yourself.*

After she had finished her sandwich and the coffee and thought a lot about herself, the exhibition and the other initiatives she had in mind to help women, she looked at her watch. It was 1.30.

'Are you Miss Subah?'

'*You?*'

The man who stood before her with his hand extended was the same man she had seen a few days ago at her exhibition. The man who had visited with his daughter and tried to get too pally with her. The creep who'd tried to introduce himself and had even touched her arm. In other words, the kind of guy Subah wanted to avoid at all cost.

The man standing before her might not have any manners, but she did. In any case, this was a public place, she reminded herself, and she had nothing to worry about. 'Yes, I am.'

'I'm Johnnie Sparks. I'm here to meet you.'

'What?'

He took a seat opposite her. 'Wait a minute, we met the other day, didn't we? When my daughter entered your exhibition and I followed her in.'

This was a setup, thought Subah. It had to be. First the man tried his tricks in person; then, after not succeeding, he stalked her and arranged a meeting without her having any clue. And now he was pretending that he had only just now recognized her.

It was best to throw him off guard. 'Are you stalking me?'

'Stalking? Look…no, why should I? You were the one who sent an email to my company and arranged a meeting—and here I am.'

'No, I smell something fishy here, mister. Tell me what you want.'

'I want to discuss what you would like my company to do.'

There was silence for a full minute, after which a waiter appeared at their table.

Subah gave it some thought as he ordered coffee. Even though the chance was slim, what if this man was speaking the truth? Her practical side murmured: *There's no harm in giving it a shot*. Subah desperately needed help, so she agreed with that voice for the moment.

He was waiting for her to begin, elbows on the table, calm, composed and formal-looking.

'Okay, the newspapers have not printed much information about my exhibition, so people don't know it is on, and I'm not being able to sell my paintings.'

'My company can promote you. Is that what you want?'

'People already know about *me*. I want them to know that I'm exhibiting my works so they can come and take a look and, if they like something, buy it. That way, I make some money and this exercise is worth it. Do you get me?'

Akash looked at the woman closely. The first time he had met her, she had humiliated him without any reason, and this time, she was being arrogant and bossy. But he was here for a job, so he decided to play it cool. 'Sure, I can do that for you. May I know your budget and when you want me to start?'

'I have no idea how much you charge, but I can spare around ₹25,000… Is that too little?'

'No, it's good.'

'Can we start immediately?'

'Why not?'

They discussed Subah and her works after that. Akash listened to her with complete attention and was swayed a couple of times by the intensity of her emotions when she described her art to him. Also, he learnt a great deal about her. In between, while she visited the restroom, he googled her and read her Wikipedia page and recent reviews. This was a proud, talented woman.

Akash had not met many women who were so sure of themselves. That was impressive, and as a supporter of equal rights for men and women, he admired Subah for it. Additionally, she was beautiful. He noticed that her gaze was determined, even though her face was delicate. She walked gracefully, and for some reason, he now realized, he seemed to like her. Was it due to the fact that she was so confident or was it because he was attracted to her? Thanks to the way she had treated him at her exhibition, the latter was not possible. So it had to be the former, he concluded quickly.

But his problem lay elsewhere. He wasn't sure if he could take up this job at all. There was still Mr Raichand to consider.

James had come to his apartment the very next day after their lunch party, and they had set up a website.

'What would you like to call your company?'

'No idea.'

'Come on, think of a name.'

Akash had looked around, and his eyes had fallen on the Johnnie Walker whisky he was drinking. He had looked at the bookshelf and seen the numerous novels that Nisha used to read. Her favourite was Nicholas Sparks. So right then and there, he had decided to combine his current passion with his late wife's passion, and the company became Johnnie Sparks.

'That's a cool name. It will work for the moment.'

Luckily, the domain name had been available, and they immediately bought it for ten years. Both had looked at the URL with equal fondness. As James had been explaining to him how the website would work, they had seen a message pop up. And since it was his very first lead, Akash had decided to take it on for the sake of experience.

But he realized now that the woman before him needed his help, or she could be in real trouble.

It was time to speak with Mr Raichand.

'All right,' he told Subah after they had finished their discussion, 'I just need to talk to my partner. I'll be back in a few minutes.'

With that, Akash left Subah, stepped outside in the smoker's area and called Mr Raichand. The phone call was over in less than two minutes. Not only did Mr Raichand say *yes*, he also said that while Akash tried this experiment, his paid leave would continue. He was a gem of a boss, and Akash wondered how such nice people still existed in the world when the television and newspapers made everyone believe otherwise. Perhaps it was their agenda to convince people that everything was in chaos. But to what purpose? He brushed this thought aside and went back inside.

Chapter 12

*S*ubah returned to her exhibition before 3. The meeting had lasted an hour.

The man had been frank and courteous, and except for his late arrival, he had done nothing to raise her suspicions. He had even told her to transfer the money only after the work had been done. That was generous, though unprofessional. He had also mentioned that Johnnie Sparks was his company name and she was his first client. He was quick to add that he had five years of experience in the advertising industry and that she could trust him. She knew she could never trust him because he was a man, but she chose to just nod. In her current circumstances, she had no option but to give it a shot.

She emailed the additional information that Mr Sparks had asked for, including a few pictures of her paintings and the literature she had so carefully prepared that described the entire exhibition, the reason for the name *Alone to the Moon and Back,* and the overall theme, etc. That would allow him to prepare an informative, impactful and truthful social media campaign. He had said he would target people through Facebook, Twitter, Instagram and Google Ads. Subah did have a Facebook account, but she had not used it for a while and had no idea if it was still active.

The rest of the day went by in a blur, with not too many

visitors. Frustrated and tired of waiting, she drank many cups of coffee and wrote a few things in her dairy.

Inadvertently, she found herself thinking about the man who had ditched her. That man was a cheap son of a bitch, and had she not been lucky enough to catch him red-handed, perhaps would have ruined her life. She'd just been waiting for him to propose when she had caught him. But now she was wiser.

It is easier to survive the storms of life with people you carefully choose to have around you.

She repeated the idea wordlessly, thinking about her father. It was possible to choose your friends and associates but not your family members.

Moody and absent-minded, she stared at her art in the large, empty hall. She was proud of her paintings, every one of them— they were the silent spectators of her tears, pains and victories. These works were the embodiment of her stories, celebrating the triumph of women and womanhood.

Scars don't define the pain you have to suffer; scars are the trophies that celebrate your survival.

These paintings were Subah's scars, and people or no people, visitors or no visitors, news coverage or no news coverage, these were the trophies of her survival and the survival of so many other women she had helped along the way.

Chapter 13

When Akash opened his eyes, Sara was sitting on the bed next to him, shaking his shoulders. He flicked the lights on, and when he turned to look at her, he was filled with alarm.

Sara had tears in her eyes, and his first reaction was to pull her closer in an embrace. But when she pushed him away, shouting in pain, he realized it was more than just a bad dream.

Half an hour later, he was driving Sara to the hospital. She had a high fever—105 degrees the last he checked—and was barely conscious. She had a red rash all over her body and had vomited while he was changing her clothes. Since her fresh clothes were soiled before he could even carry her to the bathroom, he had to change them again.

Akash was worried as hell. His sweet little daughter, the window through which he saw his wife every day, was in a lot of pain. What if something dreadful was happening to her? He shivered in fear, his hands firmly holding the steering wheel, the car moving rapidly through the empty roads.

At 4 in the morning, he pulled into the emergency parking lot of the Fortis hospital in Vasant Kunj, and followed the stretcher on which Sara was quickly placed and carried indoors.

Half an hour later, the doctor walked over to the chair

opposite the emergency examination room where Akash was waiting, and said, 'I think it's dengue.'

Akash's face was sweating, his forehead creased with deep worry. This couldn't be happening. *How can God do this to me? First my father, then my wife, my job, and now my daughter in the grip of Delhi's worst killer disease.* 'Oh no, please do whatever it takes, doctor. My daughter is all I have. Please …' His voice rose and fell as he fought with the waves of anger and fear.

'I'll do my best. As you know, she will need a lot of rest. There are no medicines for dengue. We have sedated her for now and will move her to the dengue ward for children after monitoring her vitals here for a few hours. All she needs at this point is rest and a lot of fluids, which we have already started to give her intravenously. Can you go home and get some of her clothes and things that might pep up her mood when she wakes up?'

'I want to stay here, doctor.'

After he was assured that Sara wouldn't be waking up for the next three hours or so, Akash ran to his car, got in and drove on the still-empty roads. At home, he thought of calling his mother, but it was too early and she wouldn't be able to do anything except get in a taxi and arrive at the hospital worried as hell. He pushed the idea out of his mind for the moment.

It was the first time his little daughter would wake up away from home, and he didn't want her to be frightened. He packed Nisha's picture, one of Sara's favourites, in which her mother was holding her weeks-old daughter in her arms, and both were smiling. He packed some of her soft toys, three sets of clothes, four towels, a dozen handkerchiefs and some undergarments. Then he showered and changed his own clothes, which had had a little of Sara's vomit dried on them.

He was back at the hospital in less than ninety minutes. Sara was still in the examination room, and as soon as he arrived, one of the nurses approached him.

'Mr Akash? Father of Sara?'

'Yes?'

'Please follow me to do the paperwork.'

He looked past her, partially dazed, not willing to move out of sight of the examination room. What if Sara woke up? She would be frightened at not seeing her father by her side. 'I can't. I have to be in Sara's line of sight in case she wakes up.'

'Sir, she won't wake up for at least a couple of more hours. She is in good hands here in this hospital, and we know how to take care of her. Now, please.' The nurse's voice was calm, devoid of any irritation, a talent possessed only by nurses in the emergency ward of a hospital, where death danced with life every few minutes.

Akash pulled himself together and followed her to a desk not far from where they stood. Ten minutes later, having paid with his credit card and filled out the indemnity papers, he got back to his spot, where he could watch Sara through the glass that separated the corridor from the emergency room. He felt weak, unsure and on edge.

As the sun brightened the sky east of the Yamuna river, the city woke up to an unusually warm late-March day.

At 7, Akash called his friend Rohit and explained what had happened.

'I'll be there in thirty minutes. Why didn't you call me last night?'

There was friendly admonition in his best friend's voice, which Akash didn't say anything about, because his friend was entitled to that kind of familiarity. But the fact was, after seeing

Sara in pain, all he could think of was Nisha and the hospital. He had deliberately chosen a different hospital this time, not the one where Nisha had breathed her last. It somehow seemed like the right thing to do. Even though it certainly wasn't the hospital's fault that his wife wasn't with them any more, in the deepest corner of his heart, he still held the hospital accountable.

Next, Akash called his mother.

'What? I'm on my way.'

'Mom, she's fine. I mean, the doctors are here. You can take it easy...probably visit in the afternoon, when the roads are quieter.' It would soon be rush hour, and Gurgaon was more than thirty kilometres from the hospital.

'I want to see Sara right now. I'm on my way.' She hung up, and Akash wondered if he had done the right thing by calling his mother and putting her under stress too. But not letting her know would have been far worse, as she would have gotten angry.

'Mr Akash, I'm sorry, but your daughter has gone into the haemorrhagic phase of dengue.'

Akash jumped to his feet. The doctor seemed shaken and avoided meeting his eyes. Akash's worries shot through the roof. 'What do you mean?'

'I'm sorry, but her situation has changed suddenly. Her platelet and WBC counts have dropped, and we might have to do a blood transfusion. We're monitoring her condition closely.'

'You can use my blood, doctor.'

'I'll let you know soon.'

The doctor left him alone, and the nurse came and announced that Sara was being shifted to the special dengue ward on the first floor.

At that moment, he felt a pat on his back. It was Rohit.

Chapter 14

Subah was satisfied. The ad agency idea had paid off. After the fourth day, when information on her exhibition began to reach her targeted audience, thanks to the attractive posts and banners shared online on social media by Johnnie Sparks' company, people started to arrive. The attendance for the final four days was five times more than that of all the earlier days put together. In all, twenty works found good homes and after she had paid all her bills, including the ₹25,000 to the ad agency, she had made enough to survive for four months.

In Subah's current circumstances, this was a welcome relief. She decided to dedicate half the money she had earned to the rehabilitation of the women who had recently registered with Help Forever. Her job was to find them employment that matched their skills. As for those who didn't have sufficient skills to find employment, the NGO paid for their training in areas that interested them at various institutes across Delhi.

When she returned home at the end of the final day, she gave Bala a wide smile and said, 'You are not unlucky, Bala. We've made enough to last us a few months.'

Bala gave her a weak smile. She helped Subah neatly stack her remaining works in the studio at the barsati. They then sat quietly next to each other, drinking coffee. Later, Subah ordered food from outside for a change to complete the celebration and ensure that her chief guest, Bala, had a well-deserved break from work. By the time they finished dinner, their moods had lifted and Subah noticed that Bala's smile was the widest she remembered seeing recently.

Two days after the exhibition, Subah tried to reach Johnnie Sparks on the phone. When he didn't answer in the morning, she tried later that day, but was unsuccessful once again. Thinking that he was perhaps busy, she sent him a text that evening. But there was no reply to the text either. What sort of a man didn't reply to a simple thank you message?

She was grateful for what Johnnie Sparks had done. It had salvaged her exhibition, and courtesy demanded that she show her gratitude. That was what she had been taught, and that was what she knew. But this man, just like every other man she'd met, didn't care about what she intended or felt.

Her past interactions with Johnnie Sparks flashed through her mind. At first, he had tried to throw himself at her, and when that didn't work, all he could think of when he had met her the next time—accidently, as he claimed—was how much money he could make off her. And now that the event was over and she had casually confided that she probably wouldn't have anything for him to work on for the next few months, he didn't want to invest even a few seconds to respond to her message! She was only of use to him physically or materially, and in no other way. How practical—how like a man.

But why was she wasting time thinking about him? Why did it upset her so much? Did she expect him to behave better? One part of her protested and said he was probably a nice person and too many assumptions were a bad thing. But the other part, the loud and practical part, the part that had been hurt and humiliated, screamed, *no, he's a creep and I shouldn't waste even a second thinking about him*! The work had been completed, the money had been paid, and all was over and done with.

But the thoughts stayed, despite her attempts to shake them off, and she spent an uncomfortable night.

'Subah, today's newspaper.'

'Thanks, Bala.' Clutching the newspaper the next morning, she climbed the stairs and pulled a chair from her studio out onto the terrace. Her studio occupied just a third of the roof, and the rest was mostly covered in pots, from where fresh gerberas, marigolds and roses greeted her.

On the front page of the newspaper was the declaration that New Delhi was in the grip of dengue. It was unusual, the report added, as mosquitoes shouldn't have had the chance to breed in the cold. But the winter had been milder that year, and pollution had kept it even warmer. Children were the worst affected. Since it wasn't the usual time to be careful of mosquito bites, mothers had not been applying repellant creams on their children's exposed skin. On an inside page, there was a picture of a young girl lying unconscious in critical condition in one of the city's hospitals.

Subah's eyes flew open as she recognized the girl. It was Sara. She was sure it was her, even though she had met her only once.

She shot up, and as she ran down the stairs, she collided with Bala, who was on her way up with a cup of coffee. Though both women found their balance and didn't fall, the hot coffee scalded Bala's hand.

'Shit.' Subah rushed to the medicine cabinet in the bathroom and pulled out the Burnol cream. She dabbed cold water on the affected part and covered it with the cream.

Within seconds, her mind was back to the newspaper. 'This is Sara, Bala. The girl who visited us at the exhibition, remember?'

Bala looked at her blankly and, after a few seconds, said she didn't remember.

But Subah was convinced it was her.

She felt guilty for assuming all the wrong things about why her father hadn't been responding to her calls and messages. *In such circumstances, how could he reply?*

Subah decided to go see the little girl. But she had no idea which hospital the picture was taken in, as it just said 'a city hospital'.

Half an hour later, she was at the Safdarjung Hospital, one the biggest in central Delhi, which came to her mind first. At the information desk, she was asked the child's full name and realized she didn't know. The girl's name was Sara, and her father's name was Johnnie Sparks. That made her Sara Sparks. But her father had said that was only his business name, and she had never asked his real name. And even if he'd wanted to tell her, he hadn't tried again after the way she had reprimanded him the first time. But what was the name he had said the first time? Nothing came to mind. And then she remembered. It was Akash. Had he also mentioned a surname? Probably not.

She thought about the cheque she had issued to him, but it had been made out to Johnnie Sparks Private Limited. So the fact was, she didn't know Sara's surname.

'The child's name is Sara.'

She waited as the woman punched in a few keys on the

computer. After a minute, she looked up and said, 'Sorry, there's no one by that name.'

'Oh, okay, maybe her formal name is different. Could you please check for the name Akash? That's the father's name.'

The woman pushed a few more keys, and this time looked up within a few seconds. 'What's the spelling?'

Subah had no idea about the spelling. It could have a double 'a' or a double 'k', or even a double 's'. Many parents consulted numerologists these days to ensure that their children's names were lucky. The spelling didn't matter.

She stayed quiet and stared blankly.

'What is his surname?'

'I'm not sure about that either.'

'So who exactly are you and why do you need this information?' When Subah didn't answer, she said, 'I'm sorry, but I can't help you unless I know how you are related to the patient.'

Subah walked away, sat in her car and wondered why she was doing this. Someone's child was sick, and her father and mother must be taking good care of her. And yet, she felt a pull towards the girl, as if she were connected to her in some way.

The girl was the only one who had spotted the snail in her work. Subah had had the image of a snail in her mind when she had painted it, but the other themes that she had tried to incorporate had made it impossible to spot the snail. She could still see it because it was her work, but no one else had. Except for that little girl. The girl who had deconstructed her most complicated painting. What else might she have said about it?

Subah turned on the ignition of her car but switched it off again.

She dialled Akash's number once more. She wasn't stalking him, just trying to learn if his daughter was well.

'Hello?'

'Hi, this is Subah. How's your daughter?'

'Subah, this is Rohit, Akash's friend. I'm sorry, but she is very sick. And you are?'

'Well, I'm Akash's client, and I met Sara once. She's a bright kid.'

'Yes, she is. Just like her mother and father. Look, I'll pass on the message that you called.'

'Wait, can you tell me where Sara is? I mean which hospital?'

'Fortis, Vasant Kunj.'

'Thanks.'

Subah knew what to do next. She grabbed a quick sandwich and coffee at a deli on the way to Fortis. She needed to see this special little girl and pray for her to get well soon.

Chapter 15

*A*kash looked at his daughter. Her eyes were partially open. She smiled and whispered, 'Dad, I saw mom in my dreams last night.'

Akash's throat was choked with emotion. He smiled and nodded, urging her to continue.

'She said I'll be fine soon.'

'Yes, honey, you will be. You will be... Dad will do what it takes to make you all right.'

Rohit stood by Sara's bed. Akash sat on its edge, his hand caressing Sara's cheek. Sara closed her eyes.

Once they were back outside, Rohit said, 'They gave her the platelets from the blood you donated. The vascular bleeding has stopped. I can't say she is out of danger, but the signs are good.'

Akash thanked his friend. 'I don't know what I would have done without you, Rohit. Thanks a lot.'

'Come on, what are friends for?'

They were quiet for some time.

'By the way, Akash, a woman named Subah called. She said she was your client.'

'Yes, I know her. What did she say?'

'She was worried about Sara. Said she had met her too.'

'That's nice of her. But she is one hell of a crazy woman.'

'Crazy? She didn't sound crazy on the phone.'

Akash shared his experiences with Rohit, first the incident at her exhibition and then his meeting with her at Khan Market. Fortunately, he hadn't had to meet her again, the ads on social media having been created, discussed and finalized over email.

At that moment, they turned their heads to look at a woman who came over and stopped near them.

Akash was the first to get up, recognizing Subah. He extended his hand, opened his mouth to say something and then stopped, remembering their previous meetings. He pulled his hand back.

'I'm sorry, Akash. How's Sara?'

'She's recovering. This here is my friend...I'm not sure if I should give his name—you might say that you didn't ask. He's a doctor.'

'Don't make me feel so guilty, Akash.' She turned towards Rohit, extended her hand and shook his lightly. 'My name is Subah. I think I spoke to you over the phone an hour ago.'

'Yes, you did. My name is Rohit. I'm a doctor, as he said.'

They talked for a few minutes, mostly with Rohit explaining all the medical terms while Akash avoided looking at her. He was very uncomfortable. The crazy woman who had treated him so shabbily was seated next to him and talking to his best friend about his daughter. And yet, just like the last time, he couldn't help noticing how beautiful she was.

He looked away, distracting himself from the moment.

'Akash, Akash...where did you go?' Rohit asked.

'Sorry, I was thinking...well, it doesn't matter. Could I get you a cup of coffee or something?'

'Right, how silly of me. You sit here, Akash, and let me fetch the coffee. Any preferences, Subah? Sugar, milk, flavouring...?'

'Thank you. A simple cappuccino will do for me.'

Subah had not bargained for this. For the first time, she realized she was attracted to Akash. It was so absurd. She was attracted to him like a woman is to a man. She needed to get away. Now.

But before she could act, Rohit was gone, and now she was stuck outside a special care ward with a person she wasn't sure she disliked.

Where was Akash's wife? Perhaps at work. After all, as a mother, she must have stayed at the hospital during the night. That is what women did—worked around the clock, took care of the children, cleaned the house and gave their bodies to men at night, even if they were tired. A woman's life was all about pleasing men. With that thought, she got back her hate for the entire male tribe, Akash included, and felt in better control of her emotions.

'Thank you for coming by. I really appreciate it.'

She looked up and met Akash's eyes, and something stirred inside her. Her first thought was that she hadn't been nice to him. 'Well, thank you. I was genuinely concerned. Where is her mother?' she asked, not knowing what else to say and sure that the mention of Akash's wife would make him look away from her. She smiled weakly.

'Her mother, well, she is ...'

'Here's your cappuccino. And yours too.'

Rohit was back, and Akash couldn't complete his sentence. He felt relieved. He didn't want her condolences and concern or questions about how it happened.

They chatted about this and that, Rohit and Subah doing

most of the talking. Akash kept quiet. He looked at the two of them closely and realized how comfortable they had gotten in a short span of time. Perhaps it could blossom into something more meaningful in the future.

He wanted Rohit to settle down, get married and have children. He'd always thought of Rohit as a family man, well behaved, caring, organized and respectful to women. In fact, good husband material. Yet, every time he had broached the subject of marriage, Rohit had brushed it away, saying he wasn't interested. Perhaps, given the way they were talking now, it could soon be over. He saw them exchanging phone numbers.

'And Akash, what is your full name?'

The sudden query threw him off balance, and before he could reply, Rohit said, 'His surname is Sharma. Akash Sharma.'

'Thanks. Why doesn't your friend speak much?' Subah wanted Akash to answer, and her tone hinted at her mild irritation.

'Well, Akash is not himself, as you can see. Look, I've got to be going now, Akash. Please call me if anything changes. Nice meeting you, Subah. Meeting a pretty girl like you is a great start to the day.'

He winked, and Subah smiled back. She didn't like that he meant pretty because of her body, how she looked, perhaps how she would look nude in bed—but she smiled and thanked him anyway. She didn't want to snub everyone toeing the line like millions on the planet. More importantly, she didn't want Akash to judge her because of what she said. The time had come for him to judge her because of the person she was.

They were alone for the second time in an hour, and Akash had no clue what to say. He didn't want her to ask about Nisha again, so he took the initiative of starting the conversation. 'Aren't you going to be late? I mean, you must have somewhere to be, and you can't do anything much at the hospital anyway.'

'Do you want me to leave?'

'No, I didn't mean that. But you see, the hospital will only allow visitors who are not related to see the patients after 5 p.m. Which means it will be five hours before you can see Sara. Perhaps you'll want to get back to work.'

'I know you're trying to get rid of me.' Her comment had a hint of a challenge in it, even though her voice was level.

Akash was irritated. 'Why would I do that? Who do you think you are? Ever since I have met you, all I've tried to be is nice to you. And what have I got in return? Now, when I'm asking politely to be left alone, after thanking you many times, you're making me feel as if I'm in the wrong.'

Subah felt blank. This man, everything he said, touched a nerve. Ordinarily, she would have hit the roof in response to such a verbal tirade, but today, she was quiet. Words eluded her, and she knew the reason: she had not been nice to the man seated next to her.

Akash felt bad for letting off steam like that. He wanted to say sorry, but didn't. Rather, he couldn't. He just looked away. He would no longer be intimidated by women like her.

'Mr Akash, your daughter is calling you.' It was the nurse.

He turned to look through the glass walls and saw that Sara was awake. He rushed inside, the matter with Subah forgotten.

Sara met him with a smile and whispered, 'Dad, I love you.'

'I love you too.'

'Is she the painter?'

Akash followed Sara's eyes and found her looking at Subah,

who was on her feet and looking at them from the corridor.

'Yes, she is.'

'Dad, please call her inside.'

He looked at the nurse. She nodded, indicating that it was okay, and walked out to call Subah.

'Subah Aunty, how are you?' Sara asked as soon as she was inside.

Subah placed her hand affectionately on Sara's shoulder. 'I'm happy to see you smile. How are you feeling?'

'Good. Are you sick too?'

'I'm fine, sweetheart. I came by to see you.'

'Thank you. Will you teach me how to paint?'

'Yes, of course.'

The doctor interrupted their conversation and started to ask Sara questions. As Akash took a step closer to the doctor, Subah took a step back. Now was the time to leave. She was happy to have seen the little girl, relieved that she was recovering—and that was the only thing that mattered.

She looked at Akash one final time. All his attention was on what the doctor was saying, and she turned quietly to leave. No one called her back. In fact, no one noticed her departure, and within minutes, she was driving back home.

Chapter 16

*L*axmi Sharma was sixty. Ever since her husband, Akash's father, had passed away two years ago, she had been living alone in Gurgaon. She liked the still silence of the house where she had lived for four decades. It was a temple of her family's memories, mostly very good, but when her husband fell sick and his condition worsened almost a decade ago, she had had the worst time of her life.

Her loving, caring and amazingly fit husband was reduced to a bag of bones, incapable of doing anything on his own. The shock of seeing him wither away bit by bit had broken her spirit. When, over time, he had turned into a vegetable, she had cried and demanded, 'Why, why are you doing this to me?' But in return he had just stared at her.

Not getting any answers, Laxmi turned to God. She did everything people told her: kirtans, fasts—she had even consulted numerologists and astrologers. She had never been much of a believer—more agnostic than atheistic—but surrounded by questions she had no answers to and aware that she and her husband had committed no sin, she turned to religion and God for relief. But all her efforts to appease God had failed.

Finally, when her husband died, she was filled with relief and guilt in equal measure. Relief because her husband's pain wouldn't bother him any more, and guilt because it was her husband who had died, a man she had been madly in love with. Together with Akash, they had spent a happy life. Her husband had been the anchor of her family.

When Akash had married Nisha, it was Laxmi who had insisted that they start their life as husband and wife in a new place. Young couples needed time and privacy and carefree moments. It was their time, and she didn't want to burden her only son. As expected, Akash had resisted and was supported by Nisha, as the two of them argued against leaving the house in Gurgaon, but in the end, Laxmi's persistence had won.

Laxmi had been very fond of Nisha, and until the day she was hospitalized, her darling daughter-in-law called every other day just to chat and enquire about her health.

Even though she was surrounded by loneliness and grief, she had stayed calm. Akash and Nisha visited on weekends. The arrival of their little angel, Sara, had brightened her mood a bit in the middle of the crisis.

Knowing that her son was happy with his family had given her a reason to keep fighting. But when Akash had visited her a year ago and broken the news of Nisha's stage 4 cancer, Laxmi was devastated all over again. Her questions about life and death multiplied after that, and there were times when she thought she had gone mad. She no longer had the strength to tell her son to fight harder. Both mother and son had lost. When Akash visited her—leaving little Sara at a day care, as Nisha was in hospital for most of the final two months—they just sat side by side, not saying anything, not touching, not looking into each other's eyes. They had no answers, and for the first time, they had no questions either.

Nisha's death, when it came, didn't bring any grief. Mother

and son had even lost their capacity to grieve. If there was one person who helped them survive the tragedy, it was Sara.

Laxmi had started her Haridwar trips soon after her husband's death. She would just go there, stay in an ashram, look at the Ganges and the mountains, and think of nothing. A few weeks after Nisha's death, slowly, the questions started coming back. Laxmi regained her sanity. She was in the world for a reason; she had a purpose. On her fourth week-long visit, she found the exact reason. She had to help her son and granddaughter be healthy and happy again.

Chapter 17

Subah drove straight home from the hospital. There was something bothering her. Bala's coffee helped a bit, but the problem still remained out of reach.

She went up to her studio and set up a new canvas. After spraying it down with water and painting on a grey background, she began to play with different shades of black and brown, changing brushes as she pleased. She had no idea what she wanted to paint. After a while, she stepped back a few feet and stared at the patterns and images she had formed. There was nothing she could see, but it was always like that. She just needed to look harder and longer.

Memories from her visit to the hospital began to swim in her mind. She stared at the canvas again, and this time, when she started painting, her strokes were more precise and the shades more sure.

After some time, Bala came to announce dinner and Subah decided to stop work for the time being. Her decision to stop was as abrupt as the one to start. In any case, it had been a long day and she needed to get back to work early the next day. She gathered her thoughts and followed Bala down the stairs to the living room.

Subah couldn't sleep properly that night. As she tossed and

turned, her thoughts kept returning to her visit to the hospital and the painting. Eventually, she realized what was happening to her. When Rohit had left to get coffee, Akash's hand had accidently grazed her shoulder, and for the briefest of moments, she had seen an image—of her and Akash on a beach, holding hands and looking at the sunset, their faces aglow as if they'd absorbed light and were now releasing it, their eyes twinkling at the prospect of a lovely, dark night, one that would be spent in each other's arms.

Subah sat up. Was it a dream? But she had not slept at all. Why was she having such crazy thoughts? She turned the lights on, got out of bed and looked at herself in the mirror. For the first time, she couldn't meet her eyes. The eyes that stared back were asking questions. They belonged to the person she was before she met Akash.

What had she done to deserve such thoughts? She walked to the kitchen and prepared a cup of tea for herself, trying to make as little sound as possible, so that Bala, who slept in the adjacent bedroom, didn't wake up. As she took her tea over to sit on a dining-room chair, she heard a shuffle of feet.

'Subah, what's wrong?' Bala came over and stopped near the table, her eyes falling on the cup of tea. 'You could have asked me to make this.'

Subah waved her hand. 'No, why should I disturb you if I can't sleep?'

Bala sat in the chair next to Subah's and looked at her with questioning eyes.

'What?'

'I know what's happening to you, Subah.'

Subah's eyes flew up. 'What do you mean?'

'Nothing. Just that...please don't be too harsh on yourself. Sometimes we need to let the current of circumstances take us towards our destiny.'

'Perhaps...' Subah didn't like where the conversation was going, and as soon as she finished her tea, she yawned uncontrollably, suddenly very sleepy. Whatever had been bothering her was no longer in control of her senses. She was who she was—an independent woman who would do everything in her might to save women from men.

The next day, a woman named Anita, who had been registered with her NGO and was undergoing training in a six-month tailoring course, called Subah. Half an hour later, Subah was at her institute. The subject of the call had disturbed her, and she wanted to discuss the problem the woman was facing and sort it out.

At the institute in Noida, where Anita was staying while she trained, Subah looked at her and asked, 'Why?'

'Madam, he has realized his mistake, and now he is really in love with me.'

A year ago, a badly beaten and tortured Anita had escaped from her home, where she had been raped every night by her drunken husband, and somehow reached the police station. Her husband had chased her, but with all her remaining strength, she had reached Chanakyapuri police station from the village of Shahpur Jat, where she had lived ever since she was married two years ago.

The police had called Subah, who had taken on responsibility for her, first for treatment and then for helping her get back on her feet. Since Anita was uneducated, tailoring was one of her few options. During the monthly reviews of all the women her

NGO was training, Subah had gotten good feedback about Anita. Until this morning.

First, the director of the institute had called to say that Anita wanted to quit, and then Anita herself had called and repeated the same thing. And now, meeting Subah's eyes, she was saying that the man who had raped and tortured her for two years had fallen in love with her again. She said that he had visited the institute and pleaded with her, saying he was sorry. And this woman had accepted his apology and wanted to start afresh. She now thought Subah was blocking her path to freedom and love.

'What if he does the same thing to you that he did before?'

'Madam, please, he won't. He is in love with me. While I was away from him, he realized my value. I can see it in his eyes. He has never looked at me this way before.'

In the end, when all her logic and concerns had been brushed aside, Subah gave up and allowed Anita to withdraw. Her NGO had lost money, and this woman was preparing to go back to hell. But there was little she could do.

As Subah walked back to her car, her phone rang. It was Rohit. Worried about Sara, she answered the call immediately, her mind transitioning from the institute she was in to the hospital where she'd been the day before.

'Hi, this is Rohit.'

'Hi, Rohit. How are you?'

'I called to say hi and ask how you were doing.'

'I'm doing okay. How's Sara?'

'Sara is fine, in fact recovering faster than the doctors had predicted. It's a good sign. If all goes well, she should be home in a day or two.'

'I'm so relieved to hear that! Her dad and mom will rest easier now.'

'Dad, yes, but mom...I can't say, as she is too far away.'

'Far away? What do you mean?' Subah was frustrated. How irresponsible of a mother! At least the father was there to take care of his daughter. Her anger at the mother painted the father in a better light.

There was silence for a few seconds. Then Rohit asked, 'Don't you know?'

'Know what?'

'Sara's mother died a year ago.'

That hit her hard. For a second, Subah was silent and expressionless as a stone, and then she started to shake, her body trying to keep itself from falling as an earthquake seemed to pass through it.

'Are you there?'

The question brought her back to the present, but she had not regained her senses enough to know that the question needed to be answered. Rohit repeated it, panic rising in his voice.

'Yes, I'm here. Look, I've got to go.'

Chapter 18

*S*ubah disconnected the call and sat behind the wheel for a long time, memories of her meetings with the father and daughter flashing through her mind. Half an hour later, she knew what she had to do. She needed to say sorry to Akash. She had not just been rude but very unkind to the man. But would he forgive her?

The phone rang again.

'Hi, Subah. It's me again, Rohit. You sure you're okay? I mean, I've been worried since you abruptly hung up, but I didn't want to call back immediately. I wanted to give you some time. What's the matter?'

'Nothing.' Subah didn't want to say anything about Akash or his family. To make sure Rohit didn't return to the same subject, she took the initiative. 'I'm fine, really. It's just work.'

'Your NGO?'

'Precisely.'

'Okay. Would you like to meet and tell me more about the NGO? I'm curious.'

'Well...' It didn't seem right to say *no* straightaway, but she had no idea how to deflect his request. Rohit was a nice guy, after all. What was the harm if she met him?

'I mean, it's okay if you're busy.'

'No, I'm fine.'

'Look, today is my day off.'

'Today is good.'

'Great, say around 7 at Zeros? It's a nice little place in Khan Market.'

'Sure, see you there.'

What just happened? What was this? A date? Of course it was a date. And then she realized why she had agreed. She wanted to find out more about Akash's wife.

But why? About that, she had no clue.

Later, at home, she sat in front of the mirror and combed her hair. It was 6 in the evening. She had chosen a simple full-length skirt and a conservative high-neck top. No make-up, just a touch of lip gloss.

When she reached Zeros an hour later, Rohit met her with a bouquet of roses and his best smile. Unlike her, he had dressed up for the occasion. It was a bad start. She didn't want Rohit to waste his time, money or efforts on someone like her, who had no interest in men.

Perhaps I should have turned him down. Damn!

As she sat opposite him and smiled, she reminded herself of her real purpose. It made the ordeal bearable.

They ordered food, and the white wine that Rohit insisted paired well with the dishes they'd chosen. Rohit had decided on herb-rubbed tiger prawns, while she had chosen chicken florentine. They decided to share a cottage cheese and pomegranate salad that Rohit said would go well with it too.

He seemed to be in control of the evening, very sure that it was going in the right direction, and as soon as they had finished eating, he started on the story of his life. No woman had ever interested him. But that was all going to change, as he had found the perfect person. She smiled through it all, not sure how best to start on *her* purpose. Was she being selfish, having an agenda? But didn't he have one?

When they had chosen rasmalai for dessert, she took advantage of the pause. 'It made me immensely sad to hear that Sara has lost her mother and that there's no one to take care of her.'

He replied immediately. 'Yeah, really sad. And whenever I think of my best friend, Akash, I feel a crushing pain. He was so much in love with his wife.'

Something stirred in her stomach. 'Really?'

'Yes, and now he is alone fighting a war they'd promised they would fight together.'

'I know what it's like when someone you love dies.'

There was silence for a few seconds, which prolonged the moment, the words hanging between them.

Rohit leant closer and asked, 'Did you ...'

Subah cursed herself silently for the inadvertent slip and interrupted him, saying, 'Never mind.' But her composure had broken and she needed to get it back. 'Will you please excuse me?'

'Sure.'

She got to her feet and walked to the ladies' room. Once inside, she took a deep breath and wondered how similar her situation and Akash's were.

Akash had lost the woman he was in love with, while Subah had lost faith in the emotion called love itself. Either way, they were people whose dreams had been shattered through no fault of their own.

Now Akash had Sara, and Subah had hundreds of women

she had nourished with her time, money and sacrifices. And even though those women were all adults, to Subah, they were like children she had given rebirth to.

After a few minutes, when she was sure she had regained her composure, she returned to the table and gave Rohit a bright smile.

But the meeting—or the date, which Rohit was treating it as, and she'd been playing along—had to end. And abruptly. So there would be no 'would you like to come in for a cup of coffee' opportunity. She was sure he would insist on that if he dropped her home in his car.

Subah bid him goodbye while still at the restaurant, and before he could muster the courage to say anything, she turned and left. It was rude, she knew. And Rohit, a gentleman, didn't deserve to be treated so shabbily, so Subah turned at the door, smiled again and said, 'I quite enjoyed the dinner. Thank you very much, Rohit.'

Then, as she saw his hand rise to acknowledge that, she left.

Chapter 19

*A*nita was back at the institute the next day.

Subah drove to Noida again, after finishing a couple of meetings with prospective donors for the women who had recently registered with Help Forever.

The sight of Anita, as she was brought into the room where Subah waited, disturbed her. Anita's face was back and blue. There were no tears in her eyes, neither of pain nor of sorrow. She was broken, perhaps to a point where her body had turned to stone, unaffected by any emotion.

'So, didn't I—'

Anita raised her eyes, and Subah stopped. There was nothing she could do. Perhaps there was nothing that had to be done. Except get up and hug her. And that is exactly what she did.

'I'm not good enough for him,' Anita whispered against her shoulder.

'What? She pushed Anita back, holding her shoulders firmly so she didn't fall, and shook her. 'What did you just say? You're not good enough? You? Wrong. He is not good enough for you.'

'Madam, he loves someone else. Someone who is lucky, someone he cares about.'

'Then why did he coax you back? Why did he appear at your doorstep, pleading, saying he was sorry?'

Haltingly, Anita told Subah the story of how, last evening, when she had arrived at her old home, where her husband had said he now lived alone, he'd started again with the alcohol, saying it was time to celebrate. After a couple of hours, he had turned into the devil once again and raped her, even as she was wondering if it was really his way of loving. And then, when it was over, he had rolled off, walked to the bathroom and returned with a stick. He said he wanted to punish her because even though he was now in love with someone else, his body still craved Anita.

'He is insane. We have to file a police report. He raped you.'

'No, madam. This was my fault. I promise I will never return to him, or anyone else, ever again.'

The way she said it, for a moment, Subah felt like she was listening to herself talk and that this was her own story. Subah's image of herself merged with that of the woman in front of her.

Could Subah trust a man again? Never. She'd seen proof over and over again of the things men said, did and meant.

Chapter 20

'*Y*ou can take your daughter home now. She needs to rest for a few days to get her strength back, and as soon as she feels energetic enough, she can start school.'

Akash turned to look at Sara, who sat with her back resting on the reclined half of the hospital bed. She was not looking at the doctor but at her father. He winked at her and thanked the doctor. The nurse stepped forward and asked him to first pay the bill.

When Akash returned, Sara's table had been cleared off. A small bag was sitting by her side, and now she sat on the edge of the bed, her legs dangling freely. She had packed her own stuff. Her mother's picture, which had been on the bedside table, her clothes and her soft toy, Wriggly the caterpillar, were all packed to go home.

'That's smart work, Sara.'

She jumped down from the bed and hugged him. Akash picked her up, and when he met her eyes, he felt like it was Nisha who smiled back at him.

'Let's get out of here.'

At home, Akash's mother greeted the two of them, and Sara sat with her grandmother, holding her elbow as they chatted. Sara seemed to have grown in just a fortnight. Akash was relieved that it was finally over, and together with Rohit and the fabulous staff at the hospital, they had conquered the disease.

Later, after Sara and her grandmother had fallen asleep, Akash sat by the window and spent some time trying to converse with Nisha's picture. He knew what he was doing was weird. If people saw him, they would consider him mad, but doing it gave him the illusion that Nisha was still around. Even if that was impossible and he was sane enough to know it, he felt good. Life seemed bearable when he thought of the past.

The next day, while Sara watched her favourite cartoon after breakfast, Akash turned on his laptop while sipping his coffee.

The advertising agency had taken off. It was surprising, but after Subah's job, he had done social media campaigns for two more clients. It had been tough, as he was running between the hospital and home, but he had found the time to plan and work during the night. With his salary still intact, the extra money had made him comfortable, and he was beginning to wonder how best to use it. One, he could take Sara on a vacation. Or two, he could buy a nice gift for his mother, whose birthday was in two months. Akash decided to do both.

There was an email waiting for him from his first client, Subah. He hesitated before opening it. He wanted to avoid her, but because she had visited Sara in the hospital and was now friends with Rohit, he kept his feelings in check.

Akash opened the email and saw that Subah once again wanted to hire his services for a painting exhibition scheduled for next month in Mumbai. Professionally, it would be easy, as his last promotion had been successful and he knew exactly what was required. He was fine with the same fee too. Personally, though, it would be different. After thinking about it for a few minutes, he made up his mind. He really had his hands full for the next couple of weeks, and with the new project he had taken on, he was pressed for time. So if Rohit was dating her, he would take it on; if not, he could just avoid this troublesome client and focus his energies on the work at hand.

His phone rang.

'Long life. I was just thinking about you.'

'Yeah? Just wanted to know if the hospital checkout was smooth and ask how Sara's doing now.'

'Yeah, all good, yaar. She is fine, and Mom is here too. Guess she should be 100 per cent okay in a week.'

'Yeah, with rest and home cooking, she will be fine in a few days.'

'Home-cooked food?' Akash laughed and continued, 'I already said *no* this afternoon when she wanted a pizza.'

'Great, it's just for a few days, please tell her that. And if possible, please ask your mom to stay at your place for a few days.'

'I didn't have to ask her, Rohit. She's already locked her house in Gurgaon and moved in with me.'

'That's fantastic. I'll drop in soon to see Sara and your mom.'

'Sure. Hey, Rohit, I wanted to ask you something… It's about Subah. Are you guys dating? I saw a lot of sparks fly that day at the hospital.'

'Oh, man. You guessed right. Yeah, we've been on one date. She's amazing, though a bit weird.'

'Didn't I tell you that? Do you like her?'

'Yes, man, she's my type. I want someone exactly like her.'

'That's wonderful. I'm excited.'

'Thanks. Okay, got to go now. I've got a patient.'

'Sure, by the way—'

'Hang on… Shall we do an afternoon session with James again, like last time?'

'Why not?'

They agreed to meet the following day at Odeon Social.

Chapter 21

*A*kash was working on a new job in his living room when his phone rang. It was a Sunday, and Sara had been home for three days now.

He picked up the phone and realized it was Subah. She must have decided to call, since Akash had chosen not to reply to her email.

After Rohit had conveyed his real feelings for Subah, Akash found he no longer felt bitter towards her. Subah was a feisty woman, and given the circumstances in the country today, single women had to be feisty for their very survival. He was surprised to find himself approving of her behaviour. What had changed? It was obvious—the woman was his best friend's girlfriend. Rohit had told him the last time they had met for beers over lunch. The man was in love with her.

Without further thought, he pressed the accept button. 'Hi, Subah.'

'Hi, Akash. How's Sara?'

How polite and courteous, he thought, smiling. 'She's doing fine, thank you. We're planning to send her to school in two days, probably on Tuesday.'

'We?'

'My mother and I, since Sara's mother—'

'I'm very sorry, I only learnt from Rohit very recently.'

'Thank you… Well, about your Mumbai event, when do we start?'

'How about today? Look, I want to see Sara too. Can I see her today?'

Akash thought for a few seconds and decided there was no harm in it. 'Well, sure. Let me text you my address.'

'What time would you like me to come?'

'We're not going anywhere today, so if you can make it by 6 or so, we can have an hour.'

'Thank you!'

Akash didn't give it any further thought and was consumed by the job at hand as soon as he hung up.

Ten kilometres away, Subah couldn't contain her excitement. Today, finally, she would have an opportunity to be polite and show Akash her civilized side. And also convey her apologies with sincerity. Did she have any other agenda? A small inner voice reminded her of the attraction she felt for Akash. But no, that was wrong, as inappropriate as, perhaps, Rohit's thoughts about her.

That chain of thought made her uncomfortable, and she realigned her priorities. She just wanted to see Sara, be nice to Akash and his mother, if she got the chance to meet her, and discuss her Mumbai exhibition. Her friend had confirmed that the fee Akash charged was a steal, way below industry norms. This was a meeting to get their relations on an even keel. That was her only agenda, and it seemed fair.

That evening, she wore a tight top she had not worn for ages. It revealed a bit of her cleavage and, combined with a knee-length skirt and boots, she looked younger and sexier. Since she had been dressing conservatively for the past couple of years, the pampering gave her a new high. She liked what she saw in the mirror and sat down to prepare her face.

The inner voice called out to her again: *What's wrong with you?*

'What do you mean?' she responded to her reflection in the mirror.

Your job is to help women whose lives have been ruined by men. Why are you behaving like a teenage girl today?

Subah couldn't win this argument with herself. Why *was* she behaving like this? Why did she want to see Akash? She thought about the vision she'd had of him and her the other day. The questions left her weak and tired.

She got out of the clothes she had chosen, put on a simple salwar kameez and pulled her hair back in a tight ponytail. She met her own eyes in the mirror—she was once again a woman with a purpose, someone men wouldn't dare take for granted, someone who would help all the women she could.

Her eyes were intense and her face taut with renewed focus. This was who she was, and this was who she'd remain. With that, the momentary deviation in her behaviour was forgotten.

Chapter 22

*L*ater that evening, Akash opened the door for Subah, smiled, didn't offer his hand, and walked her in after they greeted each other. The arrangement in the living room was simple—a large sofa that could seat three, and two single ones. Akash asked her to sit in one, and after she sat, he occupied the other.

'Thank you for the last-minute help on the exhibition at the Habitat Centre. It worked well for me.'

'I should thank you. You were my first client, and I'm glad my work helped you reach people and achieve your target.'

'Well, you sure know how to spark curiosity with your campaigns.'

'That's my job.'

They were quiet for a few seconds, and Subah had no clue what else to say. Usually so confident and in control of every conversation, she felt a little lost at the moment. Akash did make her feel different, and that was one fact she couldn't turn away from.

Even though she was attracted to him and fantasies periodically haunted her, Subah had been confident that she would be able to control her emotions when the time came, however strong they were. Until that moment. It was not just her resolve that was under threat—she was scared that something was transforming her from deep within. Probably it was the same spot her hatred of men came from. Akash's influence, to her agony and delight, was eroding that very spot. She had no idea if that was a good thing, but whatever it was, the change was altering her fundamental understanding of life and love.

'Before we begin, can I offer you something? Tea? Or coffee, perhaps?'

'I don't want to trouble you...'

'It's no trouble at all.' Akash was already on his feet. 'Tea or coffee?'

'Coffee.'

He nodded and disappeared into the kitchen. She heard drawers opening, the slosh of water, the click of a lighter, and some other sounds.

Where is Sara?

'Sara's sleeping. Should be up any time now,' Akash shouted from the kitchen.

How did he know what I was thinking? She shifted in her seat.

Subah looked around the living room. It was done tastefully. The furniture, the double curtains, the bookrack in the corner, the art pieces on a contemporary shelf to one side and the few paintings on the walls—the arrangement was minimalistic but refined. She zeroed in on the paintings and strolled over for a closer look.

There was one by Natvar Bhavsar and two each by Maya Burman and Samir Mondal. She was attracted to the one by Natvar more than the others. Tilting her head and moving back and forth, she examined it from all angles and found herself communing with it.

Overall, it was an eclectic collection, and even though the

painters, and indeed their styles and techniques, were different, they fit well with each other on the wall. To be able to make an amalgam of disparate pieces that was collectively coherent as a larger work of art required an understanding of art and, more importantly, of life.

'Nisha bought those when we were setting up our house.' Akash's voice reached her from the kitchen.

'These paintings are beautiful. In fact, the diverse expressions combine to create a unique art piece,' whispered Subah without turning, unable to peel her eyes away from them.

'The coffee is ready,' Akash said. His voice was polite and distant, just like she had heard it many times before.

When she turned, she saw that a middle-aged woman was also seated in the living room now.

'Mom, this is Subah. She's a painter, and she's here because I'm helping her with an ad campaign.' He paused, turned to look at Subah and said, 'Subah, this here is my mom.'

'Nice to meet you, Auntyji.'

'Same here. It's good to have an artist in our home.'

'Thank you. Yes, I'm an artist, but I'm more known for helping women through my NGO.'

'That's brilliant, beta. Tell me more about it.'

Akash left the two women and walked into the adjacent bedroom to check on Sara. She was still asleep, but as soon as he walked in, she stirred and opened her eyes. On seeing him, she smiled and whispered, 'Dad, I love you.'

'I love you too.' He caressed her hair and bent down to kiss her.

She laughed. 'Your beard, Dad.'

Akash instinctively raised his hand to his chin and realized that he had not shaved for the past two days. Since he was working from home now, he was taking it easy.

His thoughts turned to Subah. What would she think? She surely must have noticed his shabby look. But what did it matter what she thought of him?

He could hear his mom and Subah talking in the living room.

'Dad, who is Dadi talking to?'

'Remember that painter aunty?'

Sara pulled the blanket to one side and dashed out of the bed and the room. Akash straightened up, smiled and returned to the living room.

Chapter 23

The moment Subah saw Sara running towards her, her excitement found a new impetus. The young girl jumped, and Subah caught her, even though she was not sure if the sofa would topple over. She felt it wobble, but they didn't fall.

'Hey, careful.' It was her dad in the background, but Sara was already sitting in Subah's lap and asking questions.

'Painter aunty, will you teach me how to paint?'

'Yes, I will.'

'Teach me now, pleeeaaase.'

Akash stepped closer and tried to pull her away by the arm. 'Beta, she is here to discuss business. Some other time, please.'

'No,' Sara snapped at her dad in a way that didn't go down well with him, but Akash didn't say anything.

'Sara.' Her grandmother tried to get her attention but got almost the same response from the little girl.

With that, the course of action was clear to everyone present. But Subah had anticipated this situation, so she had come prepared. She opened her bag and pulled out a few small canvases and some paint bottles.

Seeing the colourful bottles and the canvases made Sara gasp in excitement. She cupped her mouth with her hands, and her eyes opened wider. For the next half-hour, Subah taught Sara the basics, and Sara began to attempt her first painting. Once she had started, Subah could breathe easier, and looked around. There was no sign of Akash or his mother.

Adjacent to the living room was a balcony, and she got to her feet to check there. Even though the sun had set, there was enough light from the adjacent buildings, and her eyes adjusted to the low lighting in a few moments.

'I'm here, Subah.'

She turned to find Akash standing in one corner, and moved closer to him. 'What are you doing standing in the dark all by yourself? Where is Auntyji?'

'Well, I…never mind. I didn't want to disturb you. Mom has gone to the park for her evening stroll.'

They were quiet for a while. Subah looked at Akash, and their eyes met for an uncomfortable heartbeat longer.

'Thanks for coming. My daughter loves you so much.'

And what about you? said Subah's inner voice. Aloud, she said, 'Sara's an adorable kid. So inquisitive, so observant and full of life.'

'She's just like her mother.'

'Tell me about her.'

'She was a flame, but I wasn't a moth attracted to it. I was a flame too, and together, we were a fire that could not be doused in one lifetime…' His voice trailed off.

Subah waited.

'…at least that's what we thought at the time.' His voice was just a whisper, as if he were talking to himself. There was hurt in his voice, and she spotted the shimmer in his eyes. This was a man who was still in love with his wife, who was no longer present in the world. If that wasn't commitment, she didn't know what was. Esteem for Akash increased in her heart.

'I'm sorry for your loss, Akash.'

He nodded, swallowed, and said, 'Well…we ought to talk about your campaign. The show must go on, as they say.' His voice had changed; he was getting back to his normal self. He walked past her into the living room, and she followed him in.

Sara had painted a butterfly. In its middle was a hospital bed. There were stars on its wings and everywhere else on the painting. These, she explained, were the people who had become stars after their death.

'Subah Aunty, which one of these stars do you think my mother is?' Sara waited patiently for Subah to respond.

Subah looked closely. There were several dozen stars, and to her, they all looked the same. She shook her head, saying she didn't know.

'All of them.'

'All?'

'Yes, because my mother was like a hundred mothers. Do you want to see her picture?'

'Well…' Subah didn't know how to react, and she looked to Akash for help.

'Beta, let's leave a few things for next time.'

'No, Daddy.' Sara took Subah's finger and pulled her into the bedroom. When they stopped, she pointed to the picture hanging over the bed.

Subah's first reaction was to marvel at how much Sara resembled her mother. What she saw in the picture was just a grown-up version of the little girl. 'She's beautiful.'

'My dad says my mother was the most beautiful girl in the world.'

'Your dad's right—your mother is the most beautiful.'

Subah was in someone else's bedroom, and it was an invasion of privacy. That was not why she was at Akash's apartment. She turned to leave the bedroom and came face to face with Akash. Once again, their eyes met for a heartbeat too long. Neither of them knew what to say, so she got back to the living room and picked up her purse in an indication that it was time to leave.

'Well, about the exhibition, you just need to do exactly what you did for the Delhi campaign.'

'Right.'

She turned to leave after thanking him for the coffee and turning down his invitation to stay longer, which she knew was only a matter of civilized courtesy.

Chapter 24

The evening left Akash feeling uncomfortable. Contrary to his earlier experiences, he had found Subah to be a pleasant and well-mannered woman who genuinely wanted to see Sara. She had even thought of bringing along supplies so that she could teach Sara how to paint. How thoughtful.

Akash poured himself a drink. Johnnie Walker Red Label with six cubes of ice. He rolled the ice around the old-fashioned tumbler, sniffed from the edge of the tilted glass and took a gulp, draining half the contents in one go. The liquid, like always, burnt his mouth and throat, but moments later, calm swept over him and he sat on the sofa, legs stretched out before him.

His thoughts remained on the evening. He was angry with himself for the way he felt about Subah. He had found her attractive earlier too, but this evening, he also found her companionable. An alarm went off in his head. He had vowed never to look at women this way again. He was in love with Nisha and would always be in love with her. There would be no other woman. Everyone, including his mother, Rohit and even Mr Raichand, respected this fact, and no one had ever hinted at anything remotely suggesting another woman. To be frank, he had expected them to. Not immediately after Nisha's passing, of course, but after a year. He had imagined them making a case, suggesting that he needed to find someone and remarry for Sara's sake.

He took another sip and remembered that Rohit was in love with Subah. 'I'm happy for you, Rohit,' he whispered.

'What has your friend achieved now? Share the good news with me,' his mother said, emerging from the kitchen.

Rohit had always been the brightest of them all. Good in studies, good in debates, sports, and in practically everything.

'Mom, this Subah, Rohit is in love with her.'

'That's great, and what about her?'

'I'm sure she must be in love with him too. They've gone on a date already, and Rohit is confident she likes him.'

'Well, I seriously doubt it. That woman is looking for something else. I could tell.'

'What do you mean?' The whistling of the pressure cooker in the kitchen interrupted their conversation, and his mother went in to adjust the heat. She was back in a few seconds.

'Well, I won't say anything more. But I know one thing for certain—that woman is not in love with Rohit.'

'How can you say that? Rohit wasn't even here.'

'I know. I'm your mother. I have seen plenty of life and people—those who are in love and those who are not but trapped with each other.'

'So?'

'It doesn't matter. Dinner will be ready in a few minutes. Set the table, will you?'

Akash drained his glass, poured himself another, and went to set the table. When done, he called Sara, and after a minute, she walked in from the bedroom, where she had been watching her favourite cartoon.

'Dad, where's the pizza?' Her hands were on her hips, and she stood before him like a boss asking for clarification about an error.

'No pizza. We're having sabzi and roti.'

'I'm not hungry.'

It took him five minutes to convince her, and she only agreed when he promised her a scoop of ice cream after dinner.

Chapter 25

The first time Rohit called, Subah ignored it. But when he called again ten minutes later, she had no option but to take it.

'Hi, Rohit.'

'Hi, Subah. I hope I'm not disturbing you.'

'No, I'm busy, but that's okay. Please go ahead, Rohit. How have you been?'

'I'm doing fine, thanks. How are you?'

'I'm doing well too.' Subah knew exactly where this was going and began to think of ways to deflect the missile when it came.

'I was wondering…I mean, if you're free…I mean, could we meet for dinner tomorrow?'

There it was. The missile. What would she say now? 'I'm sorry, but I've got an engagement tomorrow.'

'Oh! That's perfectly okay. Maybe some other time. How about—'

'I'm sorry, Rohit. I'm tied up with work this entire week.'

'Not an issue. We can do this dinner thing some other time. How about getting coffee one of these days?'

'That's possible, but I'm not sure when. Can we decide towards the end of the week?'

'Sure. Lovely chatting with you, Subah. Take care of yourself.'

'Thanks, same here. Bye.'

She exhaled after hanging up and wondered if there was a better way to handle the situation. Ordinarily, she would have bluntly stated the facts—that she wasn't interested and would never be, so please stay away. But this man was different. One, he was a gentleman, and two, he was Akash's best friend.

The rest of the day was occupied in meetings related to Help Forever. In one such meeting late in the afternoon, at an office in Jor Bagh, to which she'd been invited by a gentleman named Mr Samir Subramanian, she was in for a surprise. Samir had responded to one of the mass emails she had sent to prospective donors in the hope of finding funding. She did that from time to time, and the funds she received whenever she did kept her NGO afloat. Mr Samir, as it turned out, was a man in his seventies, a High Networth Individual, or HNWI, who had recently relocated from the US.

He liked Subah's presentation, in which she shared the details of the work she had done so far, and after some discussion, offered her a place in his vast house—part of which had been turned into an office—salary support for two staff members, and a fixed sum as funding on a case-by-case basis.

Subah couldn't believe it. This man was a godsend. But was he serious? When Mr Samir finally asked his secretary to formalize the record of his commitment as an MoU, she was overjoyed. At last, she could have a real office and people to help her with all the administrative work she'd so far been doing from her office-cum-studio in her barsati.

On her way home, she called Bala and gave her the good news. She wanted to share it with others too, but couldn't think of anyone except Akash. It was a ridiculous thought, as it had nothing to do with what he was doing for her. She was his client, and even though she had been to his apartment once, the equation had not changed between the two of them. She pushed the thought of calling him out of her mind.

Chapter 26

The next few days were hectic for Akash. Not on account of Sara, but due to the two new projects he had accepted. His mother was at home, and that took care of the bulk of his workload when it came to his daughter. As Sara resumed school, even his mother could breathe easy during the day. Things had returned to normal.

One day, Akash calculated the amount of money he had made in the past two months, ever since he had stopped working for Mr Raichand. It averaged to more than his previous salary. Johnnie Sparks was a hit. It was such a welcome relief.

He looked at the calendar on the wall of his bedroom, where he did most of his work these days, and realized that only two weeks remained for Subah's Mumbai exhibition. It was the perfect time to start the campaign. But he didn't have any details about the exhibition. The day Subah had come over, they had not discussed anything about Mumbai, even though that was what they had planned to do. And he hadn't seen her since that day.

Akash decided to call her. She picked up in just two rings.

'Hi, Subah. This is Akash. How are you doing?'

'I'm doing well. And you?'

'I'm doing great too. Look, I need to know more about your

Mumbai exhibition, the details, the place, the timings, the theme, that kind of thing. Also, I'll need a couple of pictures of the paintings in the collection you're planning to exhibit.'

'Sure… hmmm… Only about 70 per cent of my work is ready at the moment. But I see your point. Of course you need the images. Why don't you…' She paused before continuing, and Akash imagined her sipping a cup of tea or something. '… come to my apartment? I mean, my studio is here, and you can take the pictures. I could also share the other details then.'

He thought for a few seconds. 'Okay, what does your day look like?'

'I'm at my studio now but will be leaving for office around 2.'

'Office? I thought you said you worked from home.'

'Oh, yes, I used to. But now I have an office in Jor Bagh.'

'Jor Bagh? Wow! That's posh.'

'It's a space provided for a couple of years by one of our recent donors.'

'Good. So, yes, I could leave right now and be there… Where do you live, by the way?'

'I'm in Vasant Kunj.' She gave him the address and a couple of landmarks.

'Great, that's not far. I should be there in, say, thirty minutes, tops.'

As Akash drove to Subah's apartment, he wondered about Rohit. How was it going between them? They must have met a few more times, he was sure. He suddenly wanted to know more about it. Work had kept him from seeing Rohit, who had called before his day off last week, but Akash had had to turn down the invitation to a lunch party as he was really busy. And all this while, he had completely forgotten about Subah and Rohit.

After parking a few buildings away, Akash walked towards Subah's door and pressed the bell. It was a DDA apartment, and he looked around. Nothing of interest met his eyes.

'Yes?'

He recognized the woman standing before him. He had seen her at the exhibition. The woman showed signs of recognizing him too and smiled after her initial hesitation. 'I'm here to see Subah.'

'I know, sir. Please come in.' She ushered him into the living room and asked if he would like something to drink.

'No, thank you.'

She disappeared from view, and Akash assumed she had gone to call Subah. He looked around. The room was done up in antique furniture, and a bookshelf covered one of the smaller walls. Subah clearly read a lot. An independent, feisty woman with great taste in literature and art. He was impressed.

'Hi, Akash.' Subah came into the living room from the stairs at one end of the rectangular hall beyond the dining area. Her studio was probably upstairs, and she must have been working. He immediately decided not to take too much of her time.

'Hi, Subah. I'm sorry to disturb you. I just want—'

'No, please, it's not any trouble. Why don't you follow me to my studio?'

So he'd been right. He followed her to the terrace and, once there, was greeted by a sea of potted plants of all colours and sizes meticulously arranged in groups. The studio was at the end of the terrace, and they ducked in through a low door.

Once inside, he was amazed by the sheer number of paintings stacked against the walls. There were a few kept out to dry and several others in various states of readiness. To him, it looked like a place where a kid had gone crazy with colours, construction paper, brushes, palettes and canvases.

'This is my temple,' Subah declared, hands on her hips. Akash noticed she had paint on the backs of her hands and elbows.

'It is beautiful.' Under the circumstances, it was the most appropriate thing to say. She seemed happy being the proud owner of this place.

He wanted to step out for fresh air, as the smell was suffocating him, but stood his ground, allowing Subah to make the next move. She was his employer, after all, and the arrangement called for basic decorum.

Chapter 27

*A*kash's arrival had thrown Subah out of gear. She was no longer the committed woman working on a deadline. A major distraction was staring at her now.

With his casual jeans, jacket worn over a white T-shirt and unshaven face, Akash made something stir in her stomach. He was an extraordinarily handsome man, not in a bookish way but in the way he walked and looked at her. Like now. She had no clue how to ensure that he didn't read her feelings.

'It is beautiful,' he said a second time.

'Thank you, Akash.' That voice didn't belong to her. She had become someone else again.

'Well, the pictures first, I guess.'

'Sure, can you help me, please? We need to take them outside if we are to take pictures in natural light.' She turned to look for the paintings she wanted photographed, and that helped her regain her composure. It took her just a minute to decide. 'These three.'

The works were large, and the two of them carried them outside one by one. Throughout, she avoided eye contact with him. She could hear him breathing, smell some of the cologne he must have used in the morning, but kept her eyes fixed on the paintings.

Finally, the paintings were arranged side by side outside,

and Akash went to work with his SLR camera. The natural light outside was good. Subah waited at a little distance away, watching him work, moments of what she had experienced when they had carried the paintings together still trapped in her mind.

'The theme is the future of the rainbow. That's: Future. Of. The. Rainbow.'

'Okay, got it. Future of the rainbow.'

'Yes. What do you think?'

'About the theme?'

'Yes.'

'Well, I like the images it conjures up in my mind. I also liked the last theme, "Alone to the Moon and Back".'

After they had finished their tea, which Bala had brought up to the terrace along with a plate of biscuits, Subah explained the theme in more detail, and Akash made notes as she spoke. She was moved by his sincerity. They had so far only spoken about work. Later, when silence fell between them, he was quickly up on his feet, ready to go.

'If we're done here, I won't keep you from your work. I guess I should be going now.'

Even though it was time for him to go, Subah wanted him to stay and chat with her a while longer. 'I won't be working for the next couple of hours. In fact, I was wondering how best to use this break.'

'Well, you could…I'm not sure what you like to do.'

'I think we should spend some more time together so you can get to know me better. It will help with the campaign.'

'Right, but—'

'Unless, of course, you're busy.'

'No, I'm not that busy, but I really ought to head back.'

She looked at him and felt the same sway in her head that she had experienced earlier. There was something in the way he looked at her. Or was she just hallucinating? What was happening to her? She should probably just let him go.

The vision hit her again, the images all jumbled up. In the vision, they were together in some ancient time, a thousand years ago or more.

'Okay, maybe a coffee.'

It was at that moment that she realized she was holding his hand. 'I'm sorry.' She pulled her hand back.

'Subah, you're working too hard.' It was all he said, and she believed him. She wanted to get rid of her own thoughts, the images floating in her mind. Today, she wanted to believe other people, not herself.

They had reached the living room, and Bala was looking at them. 'Sir, you are right, she hardly sleeps these days. In the daytime, she's in her new office, and at night, she paints. I have no idea if she's slept at all this week.'

Subah stared at Bala, who stared back, not dropping her eyes. She knew she was right, and it was Subah who had given her the confidence to voice her opinion. 'Okay, sorry everyone. I promise I will take better care of myself.' Subah raised her hands.

'I'll wait here, and we can leave as soon as you're ready.' Akash looked first at Bala and then at Subah.

Subah dashed into the bedroom and closed the door. Without realizing it, she began to cry. It was very uncharacteristic of her, and only when the first teardrop slithered across her face and fell on her hand did she realize what she was doing.

What was happening to her? Was it really because she was overworked and tired, or was it because of her feelings for Akash?

Her inner voice whispered, with what she thought bordered on sarcasm: *Get up and go with him now. That is what you wanted, isn't it?*

She ignored it.

It was very difficult to decide what to wear. Part of her wanted to dress well, to feel beautiful; and the other part wanted her to stick to her usual conservative apparel. She waited for the inner voice to make a suggestion, but nothing came. Finally, she put on a pair of jeans and a short jacket over a simple shirt. The only difference from her usual look was that this time, she freed her hair and shook her head before combing through the shoulder-length curls.

Fifteen minutes later, they were seated at a café in DLF Promenade, not far from her home. It had taken them just five minutes in Akash's car. Both sipped coffee, and since they had already discussed work at her place, as soon as they finished talking about the weather, there was nothing left to say. As companions in a coffee shop, the two of them didn't know which way to steer the conversation.

This time, Subah took the lead. 'So tell me, what do you do when you're not working?'

'Well, I like to hang out with friends sometimes or read a book.'

'Movies?'

'Not really. What about you?'

'I like movies. But I love reading too. So, since reading is our common interest, why don't we discuss that? Your favourite books?'

'I like thrillers. They're very much like life at the moment, only more intense. You?'

'Well, I like literary fiction.'

'That makes sense. From what I know, literary fiction mimics real life; it's not an escape, like, say, romance. Am I right?'

'Yes.'

Akash thought about Rohit. 'Do you have a boyfriend?' It was unlike Akash to ask such a personal question, but not knowing what else to say, it appeared to be a good direction to take. Soon, when Rohit and Subah revealed it officially, he would wink and whisper that he knew all along.

'No.'

'Really? I thought you did. I might even know...'

'I really don't have a boyfriend. I did have one once, and...'

'And?'

What was she doing? Why did she have to go and say that? Subah was angry with herself. She looked at Akash. He looked back at her, and their gaze held, for a few heartbeats longer before she said, 'And nothing.'

'Are you all right?'

She looked away, turned to look back at him, and smiled, 'Yes, I am.' Then, after a pause, she added, 'The trouble is I remember more than I can forget.'

Chapter 28

*A*kash was taken aback by what Subah said. She said she didn't have a boyfriend. Did that mean Rohit and Subah were not together? The woman before him seemed perfect for his best friend.

Today, for the first time, Akash had seen her vulnerable side. This beautiful woman was hiding more than she showed the world. She was like an iceberg, just a fraction visible and the rest underwater, out of sight. What had happened between her and Rohit? Rohit had mentioned that they'd been out on one date and were meeting again soon. No woman in the world could ignore a man like Rohit. Not that he bothered much about dating. In fact, the only time Rohit had shown real interest in a woman was when he had met Subah. Akash decided to check with him first thing after leaving here.

'You sound philosophical, Subah.'

'Philosophical or not, I spend a lot of time thinking about people and their behaviour, desires, attitudes, weaknesses, etc. I've seen the strongest people with major flaws and the weakest almost perfect. The world is a trap where everyone suffers. Sometimes I wonder what we're doing here, everyone in need of something from each other and no one happy. Happiness, strangely, is known only to the animals.'

'And happiness, to borrow your words and rephrase them, is when you remember less and forget more.'

'Yes, you could say that. Look, we are all prisoners of our past. The past makes us real. It slows us down, yes, but it speaks to us and shows us the right path, doesn't it?'

'So your past is stopping you from feeling what you want to feel about certain people?' It was a direct question, but given these circumstances of deep human introspection, Akash wanted her opinion.

'I did fall in love once, if that's what you want to know, but he turned out to be a...'

Her voice trailed off, and Akash saw her wordlessly continue to speak. Her eyes had turned moist, and her gaze was unfocused. He waited for her to stem the tide of her emotions.

The waiter came and cleared the empty cups. Akash motioned for the bill even as he waited for her to reply.

'Thank you for today. I really appreciate your time.' She had chosen not to, and Akash thought it best not to prod her further.

They got up and started to move towards the car park.

'You're welcome. In fact, thanks for suggesting that we have coffee together, because it has helped me understand you more deeply.'

'And what have you understood about me?'

'That I haven't understood you at all.'

Both laughed at the same time as they reached the car. The tension of the serious discussion erased, Akash dropped her home, waved goodbye and started back.

While on his way, still thinking about the conversation they'd had at the coffee shop, he connected to the Bluetooth on his phone at a traffic signal and called Rohit.

'Hey Rohit, how're you doing?'

'Great.'

'Yeah, same here. Okay, tell me, how's it going between you and Subah?'

'Nothing. We haven't yet met again.'

'But you said you were going to see her.'

'I tried, but she said she was busy.'

'I think you need to try harder. I just had a meeting with her. She's someone who appears to be hurt deep down. She didn't say that, but that's the impression I got.'

'You met her? Where?'

'For her Mumbai exhibition, which is just around the corner. Today, I got the impression she was a bit down. Look, why don't you call her again and invite her out? My gut feeling is she will agree. You two will make an amazing couple, trust me.'

Rohit laughed on the other end of the line, and Akash felt good hearing his best friend laugh. 'Sure. Just thought she was putting off having a date because when she said she was too busy to take time out for dinner, I suggested coffee. But she didn't have time for that either.'

'Everyone eats dinner. Just invite her. Keep asking until she agrees. I know she will.'

'You sure?'

'Well, call it a gut feeling.'

When Akash entered his apartment ten minutes later, it was around 3 in the afternoon and Sara had just gotten back from school. She jumped on him as his mother looked on. Akash helped her with her shoes, listened to her stories from school, and soon they were at the dining table eating the lunch prepared by his mother. Halfway through, as he was listening to Sara, he thought of Nisha. How much he missed her. He pushed his chair back, walked into the bedroom and looked at the picture of his wife over the bed. Nisha smiled back at him from the picture. He felt a small hand touch him from behind, and without breaking his gaze, he held Sara's hand tightly.

'Dad, I miss Mummy too.'

Chapter 29

*S*ubah was in her office in Jor Bagh when she received a call from Rohit. She looked at the clock. It was 4 in the afternoon. Rohit had not called her for the last few days, and it would be impolite not to talk to him now.

'Hi, Rohit.'

'Hi, Subah. How are you? I thought I should call and say hi.'

'So nice of you, Rohit.'

'Are you still busy?'

'I am, unfortunately. But that's not likely to change for some time, so please go ahead.'

'Okay, well, I was thinking about dinner tomorrow. Whatever time suits you.'

Subah thought about it for a while, and a plan began to emerge in her mind. She could go on a final date with Rohit. Tell him clearly that she couldn't see their relationship progress beyond friendship. 'Sure, where?'

'Let's meet in Vasant Kunj this time. You live there, right?'

'Yes.'

'That will save you time, as you will not have to travel too far.'

'How very thoughtful!'

'Does 8 sound okay to you?'

'8 is great.'

'I'll send you the details about the place.'

'Sure, bye, and see you.'

'Bye.'

Subah got back to work without any further thought. Prerna and Aparna, the two people she had hired with Mr Samir's money, were efficient but untrained, fresh from college, and needed guidance. Initially, most of Subah's time was consumed in explaining the fundamentals of her NGO's work. But slowly, over the past few weeks, the two of them had taken a lot of pressure off her. Finally, as the dates of her Mumbai exhibition approached, she had had more time to focus on her paintings.

She received a message from Rohit the next day. The place was called Zantos, and she googled it to find the address. It was barely a few hundred metres from her home, and she wondered why she had never noticed the place. Maybe it was new.

In the evening, she left for home at 6, her usual time. After a cup of tea that Bala had prepared, she decided to get dressed. Rohit had asked for her address and said he would pick her up at 8. He was treating it like a real date, just like last time, and she felt the pressure to dress appropriately—not go the full distance, but at least look like she had made an effort. She expected him to be overdressed, so she surely couldn't underdress.

She confided in Bala.

'Subah, just be plain and simple. I think he'll get the message in the first instant, and from that moment on, he will keep himself in check.'

'Okay.'

'To be frank, you should not have said yes.'

'I said yes because he is Akash's best friend.'

'And why do you have to be so nice to Akash?'

For that, she didn't have an answer. It was a good question. She had no reason to be nice to Akash or, through him, his friend. She dressed in her usual salwar kameez, put up her hair in a tight ponytail, and decided to wait in the living room, reading a book.

The doorbell rang at exactly 8. She opened the door, smiled and walked alongside Rohit to the car, which was parked just a few feet away. The two of them got into the backseat, as there was a driver. It was a Mercedes, and she wasn't sure if Rohit owned one or had hired it just for today to impress her. Either way, it didn't matter.

Zantos didn't have a signboard. A man stood at the gate she'd thought was to someone's house whenever she'd passed it. It was clear from the moment they got inside that it wasn't.

The restaurant had three interconnected rooms, and the two of them were escorted to a table in a quiet corner. The man who escorted them removed the 'Reserved' sign from the table and eased their chairs in as they sat. The decor was understated, the lighting perfect, and somewhere in the distance, she heard the sound of a water fountain that blended quite strangely with the slow music.

'You look lovely, Subah.'

'A complete lie.'

He laughed an easy laugh, as if he had practised it. It was the moment of reckoning. Was she imagining things? Rohit might have meant only to be nice to her, just to see if their interests matched and they could become really close over a period of time, like lovers. Well, if he was trying to see if they were compatible, she could easily prove to him they weren't— surely that would be easier and less painful than her original plan. She waited for him to make the first move.

'So, do you like watching movies?'

'Do you?' she asked, stalling.

'I love movies.'

'I don't watch movies at all,' she lied. 'I hate them.'

The waiter appeared and showed them the menu. Rohit said, after a brief pause while both browsed the list, 'Would you like crabs? These people make very good crabs that come fresh from Mumbai every day.'

'No, thank you, I don't like crabs. But you go ahead, please.'

'No problem, let's have something else. What do you like?'

Now she had to say something. She suggested a couple of vegetarian dishes, saying she didn't have any appetite for non-vegetarian today, and he smiled and asked the waiter to bring the same dishes for both of them. He suggested a wine to go with it, and she nodded.

The rest of the evening was uneventful. She hardly spoke, and maintained a neutral expression, neither laughing nor commenting on whatever he was saying. Finally, when they'd finished dessert, he asked the question she was dreading, 'You don't like me, do you?'

'I'm sorry. You are wonderful, really wonderful, but...'

'But what?'

'Like I said, I am sorry. I like you a lot, Rohit, but I don't want a romantic relationship with you or anyone else.'

'Does this have to do with your past experience?'

'Please...' She got up to leave.

'Please stay.'

It was strange, but Subah thought she might end up crying. It wasn't something she was prepared to do, not in front of Rohit, not in front of anyone in the world. She was an independent woman, and she was strong. She could make decisions and do whatever she pleased. Like now.

Subah walked out of the restaurant unescorted, Rohit's voice fading in the background.

Once outside, she stopped and decided to wait.

Rohit emerged a few seconds later and smiled in relief on seeing her. He called for the car as they waited.

'I'm sorry.' That was all she could say as she got out of the car at her apartment. They hadn't exchanged a single word during the short drive.

Rohit raised his hand and said, 'Goodbye, Subah.'

For that flash of a second, as she met his eyes, both knew it was over. They were two stars once again, with their own identities and their own brightness and pathways. She turned and walked towards her apartment building.

Chapter 30

Akash, Rohit and James met at the Odeon Social for lunch the very next day. After the first round of beer had settled in their stomachs, the friendly banter shifted to some serious talking.

It was James who spoke first. 'So how's it going with Johnnie Sparks?'

Akash's smile widened before he spoke. 'Simply superb! Didn't expect it to do so well. Thanks to you, James.'

'Don't thank me. It's all your hard work. I only helped you set up the website.'

'No, that initial push was necessary.' He turned to face Rohit. 'Rohit, even before I thank James, I must thank you. It was you who put this idea in my head in the first place and set up a meeting with James. The entire credit goes to you, man.'

Rohit waved his hand to suggest it was just the done thing between friends, before nodding to one of the waiters who caught his eye. When he arrived at their table, Rohit asked for a refill of their glasses and food. Then he looked at Akash. 'Akash, it's all about talent and commitment. That's what I've learnt as a doctor.'

'But there's a third pillar too,' said James. 'And that is timing. I think we've got the timing right here. Social media campaigns are heating up. Not just in business but also politics. I think the key thing that makes social media successful is the fact that these campaigns are dynamic and can target specific groups of people, something that newspapers and TV can't do that effectively. Plus, it's really cheap and fits all budgets.'

'That is too much gyan to digest for a beer-infused brain, James,' said Rohit, and they all laughed.

Akash suddenly remembered what he had been itching to ask Rohit all day. 'So, mate…' he nudged Rohit's shoulder with his own affectionately before winking and asking, 'How did it go with Subah?'

Rohit didn't say anything. He looked at Akash's face for a few seconds, then looked away.

'Who's Subah?' James asked.

Akash ignored the question and asked, 'What's the matter, Rohit?'

'Nothing, yaar. We did meet, but she's not interested in me.'

'That's what all the girls say, my friend. You need to be persistent. Didn't I tell you about her? She's a bit messed up in the head due to her past experiences.'

'Will someone tell me who this Subah is?'

The two ignored James's question once again.

'It's not that, Akash. I know that now. Earlier, I had a hunch, but when you encouraged me, I tried to make an effort. But she made it clear to me this time.'

'But that's not fair. How can she not be interested? You're the most eligible guy in Delhi, my friend.'

'That is a friend's love for his friend. Look, it doesn't work that way. I do like her, but she doesn't like me. It's okay. I've come to terms with it. It's already forgotten.'

Akash was quiet, and seeing the seriousness of the situation, James didn't ask again and, instead, focused all his attention on the second round of kebabs and pakoras, which no one had touched yet.

When Akash returned home, he was irritated with Subah. Rohit was not just Akash's best friend, he was also a wonderful human being who was kind, employed and civilized. That woman was weird, and once again, he was reminded of the way she had behaved when he accidently ran into her at her exhibition. It was strange that she was helping other women when she was really the one who needed help.

After dinner, when Sara had fallen asleep, Akash's mother came and sat beside him in the living room, where he had begun work on his laptop. 'You are working too hard, my son.'

'No, just want to finish a few things so that when you go on your trip to Haridwar next week, I can dedicate the time to taking care of the house and Sara.'

Her expression clouded. 'I can cancel my trip and change my plans to next month, beta.'

'No, please. It is all under control, Ma. And about working hard, it's not as much as you're imagining. In fact, just today, I had a wonderful lunch party.'

'With Rohit?'

He nodded. 'And another friend.'

'How's Rohit doing? Ask him to come visit. I haven't seen him in ages.'

'He's doing fine. Just busy and heartbroken at the moment, poor chap.'

'Heartbroken? What happened? I thought Rohit had no interest in girls?'

'Well, that changed when he met Subah. But apparently, it's not going to happen, because she doesn't like him.'

'Doesn't like him? There can't be anyone in the world who doesn't like Rohit. We always thought that when he finally decided on a girl, any girl, it would all be over, because no girl in her right mind would say no to a man like Rohit.'

'But we were wrong. Subah said no. And she was the first girl he genuinely liked.'

His mother exhaled as if she was going to say something important, but there was resignation in her voice when she said, 'Remember what I told you about Subah? She's different, and her interests lie elsewhere.'

'Elsewhere? What do you mean? You've only met her once, and that too, in our house. What do you know about her, Ma?'

'I'm a woman. I know certain things you don't.'

'And what might those be?'

'I'll tell you when the time comes.'

'Come on, Ma. Please don't make this so suspenseful. What do you know about Subah that Rohit and I don't?'

'Okay, I feel she is nice. In many ways, she is like our Nisha.'

'What are you saying, Ma? Like Nisha? What do you mean?'

His mother gave him a significant look, and he was appalled at the implication. 'Oh come on! You can't seriously mean... '

'I didn't want to say anything to you. But it's what my instincts tell me, and my instincts have never been wrong about such matters.'

'That's so wrong, Ma. As far as I'm concerned, there's no woman like Nisha in the world. I will finish Subah's work and stay miles away from her once I'm done.'

'Good night, son.'

'Good night, Ma.'

Akash shut down his laptop. His appetite for work had gone. First the conversation at the bar with Rohit, and now with his mother. He entered his bedroom, flicked the bed lamp on and picked up Nisha's letter.

Chapter 31

Subah arrived in Mumbai two days before the scheduled opening of her exhibition. A local agent had received her paintings the day before her arrival and arranged for them to be transported to a warehouse near the Jehangir Art Gallery in Colaba, the venue for her week-long exhibition.

From the airport, she departed for the warehouse and, on her way, asked the agent to meet her at the entrance to the gallery. The agent, a Parsi gentleman named Mr Taraporewala, was a wiry man of around sixty who'd probably never smiled in his life. But within a few minutes, he put Subah at ease and promised her that all her requirements would be met on time. Then the two of them entered the office of the gallery to complete a few formalities and, when that was done, stepped into the area where her exhibition was to be held.

Subah was already aware of the dimensions of the exhibition hall, but she took a few moments to soak in the place. Then she pulled out the paper on which she had marked the placement of her series of paintings, along with a few other details, and handed it to Mr Taraporewala.

He peered at the paper through his soda-bottle glasses for a minute, then looked up. 'Madam, it will be ready as per your specifications.'

She smiled in relief and asked, 'Tea?'

Travelling and the anticipation of meeting her agent and seeing the place had worn Subah down. She missed having Bala by her side. The initial plan was to bring her too, but later, Subah had decided against it due to the additional expenditure it would entail. Besides, she would be worried constantly about Bala's safety in an unfamiliar city. Mumbai was generally safer than Delhi, no doubt, but a few recent incidents had hurt that image, and Subah was not prepared to take any chances.

'You like Irani chai?'

'Yes, I love it.'

'I know the best place for it. It is run by my brother.' For the first time in nearly two hours, she saw a faint smile cross Mr Taraporewala's face.

They crossed the road, walked alongside the Army-Navy building and rounded it to arrive at a café adjacent to a traffic signal. Without consulting Subah, Mr Taraporewala swung into action as soon as they were seated and placed an order in Hindi: 'Boss, make chai and bun-maska.' Subah looked at him, and he explained, 'Without bun-maska, the chai is no good.'

It was her turn to smile now.

After saying goodbye to Mr Taraporewala half an hour later, Subah walked from the café to her hotel. The hotel was a quaint little place called Colaba Nest, located on the road that ran parallel to the Colaba Causeway. She had found this small, twenty-room hotel online and booked it the day before her arrival. Easily accessible from the gallery on foot, its location in the heart of Colaba meant that she would be close to all the daily necessities.

Subah had gone to the hotel first to drop off her suitcase

before heading over to meet Mr Taraporewala. Now she picked up her luggage from the reception and took the lift to her third-floor room. The room was basic, and though she didn't have a view of the sea from her window, she could smell it, and if she concentrated hard enough, even hear the waves crashing on the boulders near the Gateway of India.

After a quick shower, she sat on the bed in her bathrobe, wondering what to do next. She had finished all the work she'd planned for the day. It was 5 in the evening, and after some thought, she decided to go for a stroll. Before she did, she ordered tea from room service, ignoring the tea maker in the room.

When she hit the Colaba Causeway an hour later wearing jeans and a T-shirt, the first thing that made her smile was the Mumbai weather. The air felt cooler on her skin, and she smiled in relief, as Delhi was already too hot, even though it was early summer.

In all, she had fifty paintings for the exhibition, and she hoped to sell at least thirty of them in the first six days. For the final day, she planned to hold a discount sale, as selling cheaper would be wiser than paying to transport them back to Delhi. She felt uncomfortable thinking of art as trade, but it was the truth, and in any case, she needed the money. When she had visited the gallery earlier that day, she had noticed that there were three exhibitions underway, but sadly, there were not many people. Perhaps because it was mid-afternoon on a workday, she mused.

Though she had visited Mumbai for work a few times in the past, this was her first exhibition there, and her real worry was how the art collectors of Mumbai would react to her work.

One good thing was the footfall she was sure would come

about organically, as Jehangir Art Gallery was listed as one of the must-see places for tourists. But if she hoped to sell her paintings, she needed serious buyers, not just tourists.

She thought about Akash. They had communicated over email a few times after she had met him at her house two weeks ago. She had called once as well, but he hadn't picked up and later mentioned in one of the emails that he was busy. All his emails were short and to the point. But what else did she expect? As far as work was concerned, she was really happy with the creative advertisements he had prepared using his photographs and the way he had embedded the theme in the overall design. The digital campaign had already started, and he had said he would send her the analytics of its performance on a daily basis today onwards. Probably by the time she got back to her room, there would be details waiting for her. She was sure of it. Akash was a thorough professional, and that was one of the many things she liked about him. But he was also a good father and, as far as she could tell from when she had visited his house, a good son too.

She passed the Leopold Café and continued to walk past the shops. The passage was narrow, and she thought every time she visited Mumbai that it was getting more and more cramped. There were people buying phone cases, artificial jewellery, scarves, etc. When she reached the Hanuman temple, she turned around and walked back towards her hotel.

She passed her hotel, walked through the security checkpoint a short distance to the right, and reached the Gateway of India. The sun had set by now, and as she reached the boundary wall, she looked at the boats, all lit up, their lights shimmering as they bobbed lightly on the waves that crashed on the boulders below her. There were people everywhere, most with extended selfie sticks, trying to capture the most they could with their phone cameras.

The awed expressions of the tourists, the sound of the waves, the cool wind and the smell of peanuts being roasted at nearby food stalls made the surroundings seem magical, and she relaxed.

Subah had nothing to do for the rest of the evening. She did have a couple of friends in Mumbai, but they lived in Borivali, and there was no way they could cut across the city to come and meet her now. When she had informed them about her exhibition, they had all promised to be there for the opening, though.

A little later, she found an eatery close to her hotel that served seafood, and ordered prawn koliwada with rice, which the waiter recommended. As she waited for the food to arrive, her thoughts once again turned to her business in Mumbai. So far, no one from the media had contacted her. Not that she had expected them to, but Akash had prepared a press release and posted it on all her social media pages.

She imagined Akash sitting at her table, smiling. She blinked, and he was gone. It was now her turn to smile. She was perhaps living a fantasy. At a conscious level, she did like him for his looks, but that was it. But somewhere at a deeper level, she felt a connection, even though it was inappropriate and one-sided. She tilted her head and smiled. Imagining him seated in front of her and smiling as they toasted her success made her blush. The feeling surprised her. She was suddenly conscious of her looks.

The waiter brought her food, and she welcomed the interruption. She changed her mind and ordered a pint of the beer that the waiter had recommended as an accompaniment, and began to eat.

Chapter 32

*I*t was the day before Subah's event in Mumbai, and Akash had decided to dedicate the entire day to giving final touches to her campaign and rolling it out in a phased manner. He had worked harder on it this time, and the fact that, between the first time and now, he had completed four more campaigns meant he had more experience. The additions included not just the press release but a few short videos and better-optimized ads that played seamlessly across multiple screens and formats, from desktop computers to smartphones and iPads.

At 10, he stretched his hands above his head and reviewed his plan. Subah must be in Mumbai by now, as she had mentioned in her last email. Akash had posted the press release the previous day and wondered if she had received any calls.

The exhibition was being opened by Mr Prakash Gaitonde, an octogenarian who was the toast of Mumbai's art circuit. One of the most respected painters in India, Mr Gaitonde's artworks adorned the walls of almost all the major museums of the world, in addition to the houses and offices of the rich and famous in India and abroad. Though Akash had read about him in the newspapers, he'd learnt more specific details about the great painter only when Subah had told him that Gaitonde would open her exhibition.

A few weeks ago, Akash had received a call from her but had ignored it and later written a short email saying he was busy. Even though he didn't want anything to do with Subah outside the customer-client relationship that he shared with her, as a thorough professional, he wanted to give the campaign his 100 per cent.

For the last few days, Akash had also been grappling with the mysterious comment that his mother had made about Subah being similar to Nisha in many ways. Even though he had never asked his mother to explain why she had said that, the thought had been nibbling quietly at the periphery of his consciousness.

He wrote an email to Subah, enquiring if everything was on track and whether she had received any calls from the media. After sending the email, he walked across to the kitchen and prepared some coffee for himself. Sara was still at school, and his mother had gone to attend a kirtan at a neighbour's apartment, the music from which he could hear even in his living room.

He sipped his coffee and closed his eyes, trying to run through all the steps he had taken to publicize the exhibition. Like last time, he had decided to use 20 per cent of Subah's money on paid campaigns to target the maximum number of people who had listed art as their area of interest on their profiles on Facebook, Twitter and Instagram.

An hour passed without his receiving a reply to his email. But that was to be expected, as Subah would be busy running around and coordinating last-minute preparations. But it was important for him to get an update from her, so after some initial hesitation, he called her. The phone rang a few times and fell silent. She seemed really busy, so he sent her a text to call back when convenient so they could discuss the campaign and any new details she might have observed after reaching Mumbai. He signed the text 'Akash, from Johnnie Sparks Agency' to keep the communication formal.

His mother returned around 1. 'Beta, here, take the prasad.'

Akash cupped his hands, and she spooned a bit of ghee-laden halwa on his palm. He ate it, then rushed to the washbasin to get rid of the grease.

When he returned, his mother asked, 'How's work, beta?'

'Fine, Ma.'

Her eyes flew to the clock in the living room, and she got to her feet, 'I should start preparing lunch right now; Sara will be home soon. How long was I gone?'

By the time he replied, she was already out of sight in the kitchen, so he answered loudly, 'Almost three hours.'

He heard her exclaim in surprise and say something that he couldn't make out, but he was sure it wasn't important. He picked up his phone to check if Subah had replied to his text. She hadn't. Once again, he turned his attention to the plan on his screen to see if anything was amiss or there was something that could be improved further.

Fifteen minutes later, Akash's mom was back in the living room. 'Son, I need to talk to you about something important.'

'Sure, Ma.'

'Please promise that you won't get annoyed with me.'

'Why would I get annoyed with you, Ma? I promise that I won't.' He raised his eyes from his laptop, adjusted his chair to look straight at his mother, and smiled.

'Mrs Verma mentioned our landlord's sister.'

'I didn't know Lucky had a sister. Is she his real sister? Because he's told me more than once that he's an only child.'

'Not his real sister, his first cousin, who lives in Chandigarh. She lost her husband in a car accident last year. She's just twenty-five and had been married for only six months. No children.'

'What about her, Ma?'

'She'll be here this weekend to spend time with Lucky.'

Akash raised his eyebrows. 'How strange. In the five years that we've lived here, I haven't seen Lucky's sister visit even once. Anyway, what has this got to do with us, Ma?'

'Maybe she did visit and you didn't hear about it. Mrs Verma said that Lucky and Paro are really close.'

'Paro?'

'That's her name. Short for Parminder.'

'Oh, okay.'

'So…what she was suggesting was that when Paro is here, we should go meet her.'

Akash folded his arms across his chest. He was beginning to get an idea where this was going. 'Ma, why are you doing this?'

When his mother spoke next, her voice was choked, and Akash didn't know what to do or say. 'Son, I'm your mother. I only want the best for you. You can't spend your life like this. Everyone needs a life partner to spend time with. What is the harm in meeting her?'

Akash was on his feet, and when he answered, his voice was hoarse. 'No, Ma. Nisha is alive—perhaps not in your world, but very much in mine. I can feel her presence; she is watching over us. Our love was forever, Ma. Please, let's not have this discussion again.' With that, he pushed back his chair and left the room, the chair crashing to the floor behind him.

Chapter 33

'Dad, I want to go to the zoo.'

'The zoo. Sure. What do you want to see there, Sara?'

'Hmm, I think…monkeys and lions…and crocodiles too.'

Akash smiled at his daughter. She had just woken up from her afternoon nap and now sat on the edge of the bed looking at him. He was in the lone chair in the bedroom, a cup of tea next to him on a side table. He had just entered the bedroom after making two cups, one for himself and one for his mother. She was in the other bedroom and had only said 'thank you' when he had handed her the cup. Akash avoided eye contact, scared that it would recommence that afternoon's conversation. So, just like he had during lunch, Akash avoided looking at his mother.

'Why a monkey as your first choice?'

'Because we used to be monkeys, Dad. Did you know that?' She paused and Akash nodded. 'I want to know the difference between monkeys and us, Dad. Because our teacher in school sometimes, you know, calls us monkeys.'

Akash laughed, and that eased his nerves a bit. 'And the lion?'

'Because lions can eat us. Dad, promise me the lion won't come out of its cage when we are at the zoo?'

'No, Sara, he won't, and even if he comes out, your dad will take care of him.'

She laughed hysterically at the way he said it: teeth grinding, eyebrows narrowed, his voice guttural.

At that moment, Akash's phone rang. He looked at the screen, anticipating Subah's call, but it was someone else. After a brief conversation, he took Sara to a park close by. As she played on the seesaw with another child, he felt someone touch him from behind. It was his mother.

'I'm sorry, Akash.'

'Oh, come on, Ma. You don't have to be sorry. You said what you wanted to, and I said what I wanted to.'

'I just want to tell you that I respect your feelings and we won't discuss this again.'

'Thanks, Ma.' He hugged her. 'I just wanted you to know that Nisha is here in my mind, in our memories, in Sara. She will always be with us.'

'Yes, I know,' she whispered, trying her best to believe her only son, not aware of the tears that were beginning to form in her eyes.

An hour later, back at home, Akash was feeling restless. It was 7 in the evening, and Subah had replied to neither his text nor his email. That was odd. He tried her number again, and this time, the phone had been switched off.

He felt a wave of worry sweep over him. Where was Subah? Had she reached Mumbai? Was there any change in the schedule? He checked the website of Jehangir Art Gallery and found the event listed for noon the next day. There was a telephone number too, a landline number, and he dialled it. The man who answered identified himself as the nightwatchman and informed him that the offices of the gallery had closed at 6. He had no information about anyone named Subah.

Akash began to search the web for any information online. The event had been listed on a few online portals, but that could be due to either his press brief or auto-generated content from the gallery's website. His client had disappeared, and he had no clue what to do next. Did he know which hotel she was staying in? The answer was *no*. Did he know by which flight she had gone to Mumbai? The answer was *no*. Did he know anyone who knew the two of them except Rohit? The answer was *no*. All he had was her cellphone number and her email address.

Akash had never been in this kind of a situation before in his life. Clients were always there, asking questions, demanding more work, delaying payments. Never had he come across a situation where his client simply disappeared. But previously in his job, including at Johnnie Sparks, he had dealt with companies, not individuals. Subah was different. She was the company, and now she was unreachable and he had no idea what to do.

At that moment, he thought of Bala, Subah's housemaid. That was a good lead, and part of his tension eased. But he didn't know her number. After informing his mother not to wait for dinner and to put Sara to bed, he drove to Subah's apartment in Vasant Kunj. Evening traffic was heavy, and the GPS showed an estimated hour of driving time.

Finally, around 8, he pulled his car up near the building, got out and walked on swift feet up to the door. The bell was answered almost immediately.

Standing before him was Bala, her hair wild, eyes red and lips trembling. She appeared disoriented, and, for a moment, Akash thought she would collapse.

He shook her by the shoulders. 'Bala, where is Subah?'

'Sir, my Subah's in trouble. My Subah's in trouble.' With that, she lost consciousness and went limp in Akash's arms.

The apartment seemed empty, and he carried her to the sofa, where he got to his knees and gently laid her down. He closed the door, then got a bottle of cold water from the kitchen and sprinkled some on Bala's face. She twitched, but her eyes remained closed. Bala was in shock, and Subah was in some kind of trouble. These two facts were clear.

Akash called Rohit. 'Rohit, Bala is unconscious in her home and says Subah is in some kind of trouble.'

'Where is Subah?'

'In Mumbai, I think. She was supposed to be there, but now I don't know.'

'Okay, I'll call an ambulance for Bala. In the meanwhile, can you do a few things?' He talked Akash through some first aid and said he would be there in thirty minutes, tops.

Akash went into action immediately. He made Bala comfortable by adjusting her limbs. Next, he wedged a pillow under her feet to raise them slightly. Then, placing his hand close to her nostrils, he tried to discern if her breathing was normal. On finding it was, he held her hand and counted her pulse, which was normal too. He found a blanket in one of the rooms and spread it over her to keep her warm, then looked at his watch. It had been fifteen minutes.

Where is Subah and what's happened to her?

The ambulance arrived before Rohit did. The siren attracted a few neighbours, and Akash explained what had happened as the paramedics placed Bala on a stretcher and wheeled her out. Before hopping in after her, he asked a neighbour to lock the apartment and keep an eye on it until Bala came back. The woman introduced herself as Malini and explained that she was good friends with Subah and would do what was needed.

Then they were on their way, one of the paramedics continuing to attend to her while they drove. Fifteen minutes later, at the Fortis hospital, they rolled her out into the emergency ward. Akash had been in that exact same place two months ago with Sara, and his stomach tightened.

He used his credit card to make the necessary payments and identified himself as a friend. Rohit arrived just as Akash was completing the paperwork and, after nodding to him, walked into the emergency ward, showing his doctor's ID. Rohit was in a white gown, his stethoscope still around his neck. He must have left his clinic as soon as Akash called. Seeing his best friend helped Akash regain his confidence, and his worries again shifted to Subah. Bala was in the hospital getting the best medical help, but where was Subah?

Around 9 that night, Akash got up when he saw Rohit emerge from the emergency ward.

'She's stable. I think she's still in shock, but she's conscious.'

'Did she say anything about Subah?'

'Yes, Subah was attacked by some men last night in Mumbai. That's all she knows. She says one of the attackers called her.'

'Can I see her?'

'Yes. Let me have a word with the doctor. Give me a minute.'

Rohit was back in just a few seconds, and Akash followed him into the emergency ward. They passed a few beds with curtains around them, and Rohit stepped forward to open the curtains of one of them. Bala's eyes were open, and she tilted her head to look at Akash. She tried to sit up, but Akash waved her back down.

'Sir, my Subah's in danger. Those men will kill her!'

'Which men, Bala? Can you tell me what happened?'

'First, a man called and said she'd been kidnapped.'

'Did he call you on your mobile phone?'

'No, the landline. Then, before I could say anything, he hung up. I immediately called Subah's phone, and the same man answered and said I should wait for instructions. Then he hung up.'

The two men looked at each other.

'I didn't know what to do,' Bala continued. 'My Subah, who's been helping all of us, has become a victim. I never imagined that was even possible. How can God do this to her? She's a goddess herself, sahib.'

'Do you know where she was planning to stay in Mumbai?'

'She said a hotel, but not the name.'

'What happened after that?'

'Nothing. I kept waiting, but no one called. After a while, I called Subah again. That time, her phone was switched off. Sahib, please do something. Please save her life. Why have you brought me here? I'm fine; it is my Subah who needs help.' Rohit placed a hand on her shoulder, and she screamed, 'Help my Subah. God, please help my Subah!'

The doctor came in and stared angrily at Akash and Rohit. They walked out, and Rohit explained, 'The woman is still in a state of shock, and hysterical. It's possible that what she's saying isn't entirely true. Part of it might be hallucination.'

'I think we need to do something.' Akash looked at Rohit.

'She's your client, not mine.'

'Come on! I know you're angry with her, but we need to help her; it's the human thing to do.'

'Right.' That was all he said.

'Look, thank you for today. Sorry you had to leave your clinic.'

'To tell you the truth, I was seeing my final patient of the day. So it was no trouble. In any case, what are friends for?'

'Yes.'

'As doctors, we have to rush to attend medical emergencies. That is our oath.'

'Still, thanks. Now...I have no idea what to do next.'

Chapter 34

Subah got up from her chair. The air in the Colaba police station was stifling, the light dim and the furniture dark and smooth with overuse.

The stranger in whose arms she'd lost consciousness was still seated beside her, the inspector busily recording his statement.

It was Subah who had filed the FIR against the two men who had attacked her. Had she not been able to use her mind and escape in the nick of time, she would have been dead by now. Even though more than five hours had elapsed, she still shivered at the thought.

Earlier in the afternoon, when she was returning from the gallery, she had felt a handkerchief cover her face from behind. As she was pulled into darkness, she remembered kicking out at whoever it was. She had also screamed, though she wasn't sure if any sound had escaped her throat.

When she had regained consciousness, Subah had seen one of them out of the corner of her eye. He was calling a number using her phone. Perhaps he'd just dialled the number that was saved as 'Home'. She heard Bala's faint voice, and it was at that moment that she realized she'd been kidnapped.

The two men were sitting on the floor about ten feet away, drinking alcohol. Music played on a small radio next to them.

Her hands and feet were tied and her mouth taped shut. She vaguely remembered the gruesome Shakti Mill rape case in Mumbai and closed her eyes.

She was in an old building that seemed to be under major renovation. Or maybe it was awaiting demolition. Whatever the fate of the building, Subah was sure she was going to die there. But as always, she was determined not to go down without a fight.

A little later, she heard a shuffle of feet and opened her eyes. One of her captors was now standing over her. 'We want money. Twenty lakh in cash and we'll set you free.'

With this, the man removed the tape from her mouth. Careful not to provoke him, she looked at him closely. He was around thirty, his face covered in open sores and his hair matted. A strange smell came from him. She tilted her head and turned her attention to the other man. He was looking at one of the walls, not moving, his eyes out of focus.

These men were drug addicts without a doubt, and if she kept her wits about her, Subah could trick them and escape. The question was how. She could barely move an inch. 'I'll arrange for the money, just let me go.'

His face lit up. 'Where's the money? I want money.'

It was time for action. A plan began to form in her mind. There was only one way out of this, and that was to face her enemies and fight them. Subah was not the kind of person who waited for a white knight to come rescue her. A hero of sorts. Her life was not a movie, and she didn't need the help of anyone when it came to protecting herself. She decided to fight these two men, whatever the consequences.

'I need three things first.' She really only needed two and

expected the man before her to bargain and say, 'You will get only two.'

But it didn't go that way.

The man swung his hand in a sudden fit of anger, and when it came down, it hit Subah's jaw. Her body arched in the air, and she fell on her side. A wave of pain ran through her body like an electric shock. She couldn't even scream.

'You don't need anything. We need money.' The man was out of breath from the effort and his anger. 'You hear me? We want money and we want it now.'

This time, she looked him in the eye and said, 'I'll give you the money, but it is in Delhi.'

'Delhi?' He seemed confused and turned around to look at his stoned partner.

Was this the moment? What if she just rammed into him, wriggled out and, if she found stairs near the door, rolled down them? There must be people down there somewhere.

No. It was a bad plan. She needed a better grip on the situation. Brute force would not help here. She needed to use her brains. 'I'm from Delhi. If you let me use my phone, I can ask someone to bring the money by plane. He could be here in less than three hours.'

'No!' he shouted once again, and raised his hand to hit her, but stopped. She could see him thinking, but his drug-blunted brain was not able to decide anything.

'May I go to the toilet?'

His mouth rounded to say *no*, but again he stopped. She could see he was thinking, *Why answer everything with a no?*

'May I?'

'Okay.'

'Please untie my legs.'

He paused once again.

'Leave my hands tied. That way, you don't have to worry, as I can't go anywhere.'

He untied her legs and pointed towards a corner of the room. There was no toilet there. It was clear he wanted her to face the wall and relieve herself.

But now Subah had what she needed. Now she had a slight chance. She just needed the perfect moment. She walked to the corner and sat down facing the wall. Nothing happened for a few minutes, and then she heard feet approaching from behind.

Since her hands were tied behind her, she had only one weapon. When a hand touched her shoulder, she spun around and rammed her head with all her power into the nose of the person who stood behind her. He went crashing down.

She saw the other one break from his trance and run towards her. She waited for him to charge and jumped to her right at the final moment, her eyes locked with her assailant's. The man crashed into the wall.

When Subah jumped to her right, she landed on her feet and was successful in keeping her balance. Had she fallen with her hands tied behind her back, she wouldn't have been able to easily get up on her own.

Now Subah dashed to the exit, which was just a door frame. Behind her, she heard one of them start chasing her. Time was critical.

There were stairs in front of her, and she jumped down them two at a time. She lost her balance as she reached the bottom, and instead of preventing herself from falling, used her momentum to help tumble her body towards the road outside. She finally collapsed at the edge of the main door and used all her might to heave herself forward to topple onto the road two feet below.

When she was picked up by a man moments later and people began to close in on the two of them from all sides, she lost consciousness. She knew it was due to the relief.

Subah's eyes opened, she didn't know how much later, and she felt the movement of a vehicle. Her hands were free. How long had she been out?

She looked at the man who sat next to her. He smiled weakly and said, 'My name is Santosh Kamble. We're in an ambulance on the way to the hospital.'

After receiving first aid at the hospital and resting for a few hours, she was now at the police station to make a formal report. The two men had been arrested, and both were still in the hospital. One of them was in critical condition, and she had overheard the policemen say that the doctors said he might not survive. Subah silently hoped both of them would die.

She had no idea where her phone was at the moment. Perhaps it was still at the crime scene. There was something vitally important that she needed to do. Something involving her phone. But her mind wasn't clear and she couldn't think just what it was. She turned to look at the man who had so far only told her his name. Who was he? Did he have a family?

There was a mirror in one corner of the police station, and when she first arrived, she'd looked at her reflection. Even in the dim light, she noticed that her eyes were wide, still filled with horror and alarm, but her shoulders were square. She was someone who had refused to be broken. She had rescued herself, and she knew that the event had altered something deep inside.

Am I really the Subah of yesterday?

An hour later, Mr Santosh Kamble accompanied her in a police jeep to the hotel. They were quiet during the ten-minute ride. No words were required. They knew each other's names, and that was enough. How useless words were, Subah realized for the first time. He said goodbye to her at the reception desk, pointed out the armed sentry stationed outside, gave her his business card and walked out.

When Subah got back to her room, she took the medicine they'd given her at the hospital and felt drowsiness pull her in. But the images of that afternoon were too bright in her mind, and she sat on the bed with her eyes wide open, staring at the door. It was 9 at night, and she had not eaten anything since morning. She was not aware of that, however. She was not aware of anything. All she knew was that she had to wait. For what, she had no clue.

Chapter 35

*A*kash was finally able to get through to the Colaba police station after returning home around 10 and was briefed on the incident. When he explained his association with Subah, they gave him the hotel's number. He called it immediately and asked to speak to her. The receptionist transferred the call to her room, but no one answered. He called the police station again and explained the situation, saying that Subah was not well enough, perhaps, to be in a hotel room on her own. But the policeman on the other end of the line said that the decision was made by the doctors, who had said that the victim could return to her lodgings.

He was frustrated. His client was in a city where she didn't know anyone, hurt and entirely on her own in a hotel room. According to the police and doctors, the armed guard who stood outside her hotel was guarantee enough that she would feel normal soon. How absurd.

'Dinner is ready, beta.'

Akash was sitting on a dining room chair, his head in his hands. Sara was asleep in the bedroom. When he had arrived home a few minutes earlier, his mother had opened the door, but no words were exchanged before she returned to the bedroom to put Sara to sleep.

Akash raised his head and began to explain the situation to his mother in detail. First about Bala and then Subah.

After he had finished, she said, 'Beta, I think you should go to Mumbai and ensure her safety. That's who we are. And from what little I know of Subah, that's who she is as well. She is not just your client, Akash, but someone who has already been to our house, someone who was concerned when Sara was sick. Just because she doesn't like Rohit doesn't mean we should treat her as if she is a bad person. And let's not forget the most important thing...she has helped hundreds of helpless women through her NGO.'

Akash gave it some thought. His mother was right. This was purely a humanitarian case. He was worried that Subah was still in danger.

After dinner, he booked himself on the next flight to Mumbai and left with an overnight bag. His mother waved goodbye from the door. The time was almost 11 at night.

Akash landed in Mumbai at 1.30 in the morning and hired a cab straight to the hotel. The usually one-hour drive was covered in just thirty-five minutes on the empty roads. As the cab passed the Jehangir Art Gallery, he turned to see the billboard that announced the opening of Subah's exhibition later that day.

At Colaba Nest, the receptionist was asleep but woke up as soon as Akash tapped on the wooden counter with his knuckles. Outside, the policeman was awake and had stared at him without a word as he went inside through the swinging doors.

'Good morning, sir?'

'Which room is Subah Madam in?'

The receptionist's eyes opened wide, and he pointed towards the entrance. 'Sahib, you have to get permission from the policeman outside.'

This was frustrating.

Akash exhaled and spoke in a fake official voice that didn't belong to him. 'I'm that policeman's boss. My name is Akash. Here, take a look at my agency card.'

He flashed his old ID card from when he had worked for Mr Raichand, as he was still carrying it in his wallet. Before the receptionist could focus his eyes properly to read it, Akash pulled his hand back and pocketed the card.

'I want to see her now. *Now.*'

The man hesitated while Akash glared at him. Talking with the armed guard outside was not a problem, except that Akash knew he wouldn't allow him to see Subah unless someone higher up approved. And at that hour, everyone would be asleep. He felt bad about the lie, but he desperately needed to see that Subah was safe.

The receptionist dropped his eyes and said, 'Room 303.'

'I want your master key.'

The receptionist dug his hands in his pockets and handed him a plastic card.

Akash pressed the lift button and waited, his heart beating wildly.

How was Subah?

Why was she not answering her phone?

Who had attacked her?

What would happen to the exhibition now?

Where were her paintings?

Questions were still running through his mind as he got out of the lift and went to the door of Room 303. First, he knocked lightly. The door remained closed. He tried again after a few moments. No response.

Akash used the master key to open the door. He walked in and came to an abrupt halt when he reached the middle of the room. There was someone sitting on the bed. He found the light switch, turned it on and looked at the person on the bed. It was Subah. His first impression was that she had lost her mind. She stared directly at him through unblinking eyes but didn't seem to recognize him.

'Subah.'

Still no response.

'Subah, it's me, Akash.'

She inhaled sharply, and the muscles on her face twitched.

He walked closer and sat down beside her.

'Where am I?' she asked.

'You're in your hotel room in Mumbai, and I have come from Delhi to see that you're safe. How are you feeling now?'

'You're not Santosh Kamble.'

'No. Who is Santosh Kamble?'

'He is a good soul. I want to see Santosh Kamble.'

Akash didn't know what to say. He just stayed quiet and looked at her closely. There were bruises on her face but no major external injuries. He was relieved at that. Perhaps she was still in shock. On the bedside table were a prescription and a few pill bottles. He picked up the paper and read the diagnosis: PTSD. He knew what it meant: Post Traumatic Stress Disorder. He had been diagnosed with it when Nisha had passed away. The antidepressants had helped, but mostly, it was the presence of Sara and his mother that had allowed him to make it through that most difficult period of his life.

Where were Subah's parents? Did she have a brother or a

sister? Friends? Once again, he realized how little he knew her. There was Bala, of course, but she, too, was in hospital.

'Subah, Mr Kamble will come for a visit later. I'm Akash; I'm here to help you.'

Her eyes moistened when she heard him. With that, the frigidity of her expression changed, and he thought he saw a hint of a smile. Or was he imagining things, since that was what he wanted to happen? He wanted her to come out of her daze. He wanted her to speak, to recognize her surroundings, even to curse and cry.

'Akash, oh! Where were you? I was thinking about you when those men, those…' Her voice trailed off, and she seemed to return to her frozen state.

He had to take her thoughts off where they were leading her. Perhaps the best thing was to mention something he knew she really liked. *Sara*, he thought. 'I was just with Sara in Delhi, Subah. She sent her love.'

'Sara, the lovely child.' This time she really smiled. It was only for a brief moment, but the memory had stirred something inside her. 'Thank you, Akash.'

She laid her head on his shoulder, and for a moment, Akash didn't know what to do. Then he placed his hand on her head.

After five minutes, he tilted his head and realized that she had fallen asleep. He gently laid her back on the bed and spread the blanket over her, then closed the door and took the lift downstairs.

The receptionist's head was lolling, but he sat upright on seeing him. Akash ignored him and walked outside, heading towards the Gateway of India, where dawn was just breaking. He stood there for about an hour, thinking about life, death, ambition and love. He thought about Nisha and wondered what her reaction would be to all this. Would she have approved of him helping a woman in distress? Of course she would have. Just like his mother said: *This is who we are.*

When he finally got back to Subah's room, he realized that she was still sleeping. Now was the time to consider more important decisions. What about the exhibition? On his way back, he had booked the room adjacent to Subah's for himself. He returned to his room, showered and got dressed in fresh clothes. Even though he had not slept at all, quite surprisingly, he wasn't tired.

Chapter 36

*I*t took them fifteen minutes to get her to talk. At first, all her answers were one-word, and then slowly, she started to form full sentences.

It was 9 in the morning, and in addition to Akash, the inspector-in-charge of Colaba police station, a woman constable and a lady doctor from Bombay Hospital sat around her in her room.

After a while, the doctor signalled to Akash to accompany her outside into the corridor. 'She is fast returning to normal. Who are you? Her husband?'

'No.'

'Partner?'

'No.'

'Friend?'

'No.'

'Then?'

'Well, she is my client.' He explained the exhibition and his involvement in its promotion, and she nodded.

'Today is the first time I've seen her. Yesterday, she was attended by someone else.'

'Doctor, how could your hospital just send her here to stay on her own in her condition?'

'I'm surprised too. My understanding is that she was better yesterday. Sometimes, there is a delay in the shock taking root. Anyway, until someone from her family comes and takes over care of her, you need to be careful. She's suffering from PTSD, and its effects can last for up to a month.'

'I'll do the best I can.'

'Great. She is on antidepressants at the moment. She must continue them.'

With that, the doctor left and Akash returned to Subah's room, only to find that she was in the bathroom and the inspector and female constable were chatting in hushed voices. They stopped abruptly and looked up when they heard him coming.

'Mr Akash. We'll continue to post a constable outside for a few days. Do let me know if you need any other help.'

'Where are the people who did this to her?'

'In the hospital. One of them died this morning. Complications due to a drug overdose and the blow he received on the nose from Subah's head, which caused profuse bleeding.'

'And the other?'

'He is recovering and is out of danger, but the law will take care of him. We will ensure that.' The Mumbai police force, Akash knew, was one of the most efficient in the country, and he didn't doubt their ability. 'Here is my direct number if you need anything.'

They got to their feet, shook his hand and left, leaving Akash alone in Subah's room. He wondered what to do next. Perhaps he needed to speak to Rohit, fill him in on all the details and find out how Bala was doing.

Before he could call, Subah emerged from the bathroom.

She had washed her face, and he got a whiff of soap as she passed him.

'Subah, I'll be in my room. It is adjacent to this one. Room 304.' He moved towards the door and turned to look at her, his hand raised for a reassuring farewell.

'Please, don't go...' She raised her eyes and paused.

Akash imagined many questions in them. 'Okay, I won't. Would you like anything to eat?'

'No.'

'Coffee?'

She didn't say anything, and Akash, taking that as a yes, reached to pick up the intercom.

'Two coffees, please.'

Chapter 37

Subah felt clearer in the head. She looked at Akash. The first time she had seen him in the room, he'd been nothing but a blur. She was drifting at that point, not aware of where she was or who she was. It was an endless ocean, and she was on a wooden plank, adrift in the rain and storm. She was holding on to the plank with all her might, even though she knew she would eventually be consumed by the sea. And then a voice reached her. She had heard that voice before. In the vast ocean, there was someone calling out to her. She had looked towards him and recognized him. The ocean around her began to dry up, the wind slowed and the rain stopped. Within minutes, she realized she was in a room, a hotel room, and Akash stood before her. He'd reminded her of Sara, the little girl who could interpret her paintings, and she'd been so relieved that she put her head on his shoulder and slept. That time, there had been no bad dreams. In fact, she hadn't dreamt of anything at all.

Cleaning up and washing had made her feel better. As she emerged from the bathroom, she realized that everyone had left. Everyone except Akash. Yes, she wanted that coffee, and she wanted to have it with him.

Sitting close to Akash, the pain in her head began to fade. As her reasoning and understanding of her surroundings got better, her first feeling was of being overwhelmed by the fact that Akash had taken the trouble to come and see her in Mumbai.

They sipped their coffee in silence, and she avoided looking directly at him. But the fact that he was there in the periphery of her vision gave her a feeling of comfort and safety.

'How are you feeling now?'

'I'm better. Thank you.'

'I'm happy that you're feeling better. You need to take your medicines now.'

'I will. Thanks!'

'About the exhibition...' He paused before continuing, 'The best thing would be to postpone it.'

Yes, the exhibition. The real purpose of her visit. It was urgent that she speak to Mr Taraporewala. When was the exhibition? Today?

'Where is my phone?'

Akash looked around and joined her search. Her phone was nowhere to be found. After five minutes, they gave up. 'You can use mine.'

'I need to speak to Mr Taraporewala. But I saved his number on my phone. Damn!'

'Who is he?'

'My local agent here, who is helping me.'

'The gallery might have his number then.'

'I think so.'

Akash googled the gallery's number and spoke to someone who gave him Mr Taraporewala's number. He dialled it and handed over the phone to Subah.

'Yes, it's me, Mr Taraporewala. Yes, no, I lost my phone.

I'm hoping to be there. What time is it? Wait, wait…okay, I'll be there.'

She returned the phone to Akash and said, 'Akash, the exhibition opens in an hour. Where did the time go? I must hurry up.'

She got to her feet, swayed and lost her balance. The dizziness caught up again, and she grabbed the hand that Akash extended. Before she knew it, she had wrapped her arms around him. He was like a pillar, something she needed to hold on to to stop herself from falling.

It felt strangely familiar to be holding him so close. She felt his energy seep through her skin. She felt his breath, and the images began to come to her again. Of them together in a jungle, centuries ago. By a lake, eating food near a campfire.

He gently moved her arms away after a few minutes and made her sit down. 'I don't think it's a good idea to go anywhere now. You need to rest.'

Subah sat and looked at him. Even though her exhibition was only minutes away and she had no idea what its fate would be, given her condition, all she could think of at that moment was Akash. This man had taken the trouble to come to Mumbai when he realized she was in danger. Clearly, he cared about her.

Holding him had upset the chemical balance in her body, and she was surprised to realize that she was aroused. She felt excitement and guilt in equal measure at the thought. But she allowed the excitement to eclipse the guilt and continued to think about him. The man was in front of her now, and all she wanted at that moment was to be with him.

'Why don't you rest and let me run by the gallery to see what the best course of action is?'

As soon as she nodded, not knowing how best to answer the question, he was gone. She recalled she had to call someone, someone she deeply cared about. But the question was who?

Chapter 38

As Akash walked towards the Jehangir Art Gallery, his mind was on Subah. He was happy with the speed at which she was recovering, but there was something making him uncomfortable. First, it was what his mother had said, and now, the way she had looked at him and held him. Clearly, for her, he was more than just someone she was doing business with. And the fact that he was here in Mumbai had made her believe that he cared for her too. Which was untrue. He cared for her no more than he would for any woman in danger. She was just like any other woman he knew in his professional life.

Akash realized that he must do something to let her know of his real feelings so she'd stay away. But the question was how. In any case, this was not the right time, as her psychological condition was very delicate.

When he arrived at the gallery, Mr Taraporewala was waiting for him. The two men introduced themselves.

Akash explained Subah's condition and added, after a pause, 'I would like you to cancel the event. Under the circumstances, that would be the best thing to do.'

'I'm very sorry to learn about the attack on her. But I also feel proud of how she fought with those criminals and got them arrested. I don't think cancelling the exhibition is a good idea.

She won't get another spot in this gallery for two years. And what about the expenditure she has already incurred? Add that to the cost of wrapping it up now and taking these fabulous works back to Delhi.'

'Right, but there's nothing we can do now, is there?'

'Let me think.' He walked away, scratching his long nose, turned and was back by Akash's side in less than thirty seconds. 'I think we should go ahead. She need not come here if she can't. I'll handle everything. For the works that sell, I'll arrange for the money to be put in her bank account. I have her details.'

'But what about the opening? How can an exhibition open without the artist? Has it been done before?'

'It's not the norm, but yes, it has been done before. As her agent, I'll be there. You can be present too, to answer people's questions, since you work for her.'

Akash felt mildly irritated. He wasn't Subah's employee in the way Mr Taraporewala thought. He was just helping her. But he stayed quiet. The plan made sense. Fifteen minutes later, after he was given a tour of the exhibition and had seen its state of readiness, he thought it made perfect sense.

'Great, then. Let me have a word with Subah.' He stepped to one side and called the hotel. The receptionist transferred his call, and this time, Subah answered after just one ring.

'How are you feeling now?'

'Better.'

'Okay, so Mr Taraporewala says we should go ahead with the exhibition. The opening is in twenty minutes. I'll be here, and so will be Mr Taraporewala. He said he would handle everything and everyone, including Mr Gaitonde.'

'I'm not sure I fully understand what you're saying, Akash.'

He realized he had spoken too fast and given her far more details than her mind could process. After all, she was on antidepressants and suffering from PTSD. He repeated the information slowly and cut out half the details.

'But that's not possible. I have to be there, Akash. Those are my works.'

'You have to trust me, Subah. Under the circumstances, this is the best course of action. Everything is under control. Please just rest. I'll be back as soon as I can.'

'Of course. I trust you, Akash.'

He hung up.

By the time he got back inside, a few people had gathered and Mr Taraporewala introduced him.

A young girl who said she worked for *Mid-Day* was the first to speak to him. 'I've been calling Miss Subah since yesterday, but she hasn't answered.'

Another man joined them and said, 'I'm from the *Afternoon*—it's a tabloid like *Mid-Day*—and I've been calling since this morning too.'

Akash understood two things from this. One, he should replace the telephone number on all the social media postings with his own, since her phone was untraceable, and two, he should try to get a new number for Subah ASAP. 'Look, I'm sorry. I'm from her team. Actually, she lost her phone.'

'But where is she now?'

'Hmm...she's not feeling well, so she won't be here today.'

'She won't be here to open her own exhibition? Does Mr. Gaitonde know?' It was the woman from *Mid-Day*.

'I believe he does, and if not, Mr Taraporewala will soon let him know.'

After a while, Mr Gaitonde walked in. For a man his age, his back was straighter than most, his face unwrinkled and radiant. His long hair reached his shoulders, the curls shaking as he moved. He wore a white kurta, faded jeans and Kolhapuri chappals. His cleared his throat, and as he started to speak, Akash was surprised by the way his eyes sparkled. Mr Gaitonde thanked everyone who had gathered and informed them why Subah was not there. There was silence as he described what he had learnt from the police.

'As a Mumbaikar, I hang my head in shame today. Subah's agent, Mr Taraporewala, informed me that she wanted to cancel the exhibition, but he persuaded her to believe in us, believe in the love and healing of Mumbai. When he called me and said Subah wouldn't be present today, I informed him that I'd still be here for her. We are all artists. There is no senior or junior, no more talented or less talented, no more successful or less successful. We live in a division-free world, and that is how it should be. Look at these works. These are stunning pieces of art. Take a look, spend time with these thoughts on canvas and see how they engage you. I'm happy today that despite the evil present in our society, artists have the power and depth to go on. I salute the spirit of Subah as much as I salute the spirit of the Mumbaikar who helped her.'

Everyone clapped, and it seemed to continue longer than usual. There were about fifty people—the media, art lovers and a few curious bystanders.

Akash was surprised that so many people from the media had turned up. His press release and the marketing had surely hit the right notes. Or—he stopped himself from taking all the credit— was it because of the celebrated Mr Prakash Gaitonde's presence? Perhaps it was the latter, or a combination of the two.

No sooner had Mr Gaitonde stopped talking, the murmurs started. There was more interest in what had happened to Subah than in her paintings. It wasn't a development Akash was uncomfortable with, as he was aware that it would eventually make their campaign stronger. The worst was behind Subah, and now she deserved all the attention she was getting, by hook or by crook. Though he was always ethical in his career, both with Mr Raichand and now as the owner of Johnnie Sparks, he knew very well that publicity of any kind never hurt.

Everything seemed to be in place, and the cluster of people who had gathered at the centre of the exhibit hall began to drift towards the paintings. Akash joined them and focused on the paintings one by one. One thing that hit him was the lack of colour. This was peculiar, as the collection was called *The Future of the Rainbow*. Earlier, at Subah's house, he had only seen part of her collection, and although those were all black and white, he'd been hoping that she would add some colourful ones later.

Each painting was accompanied by a couple of lines of explanation that helped in interpretation. He paused and read what was written below one of them.

Love is not an anchor, it is propulsion, the courage to stem the tide, cut through ocean currents and face the storm together.

But as far as he could see, there was no anchor, no storm, no tide, and no people in the painting. All it had was two leaves turned grey, perhaps by decay, fallen near a tree, the trunk of which was partially visible. The leaves were connected, and an owl looked down from the sky, its eyes narrow and full of its signature alarm.

Akash moved to the next one.

Two people in the same room can be light years apart. The human mind is such a big universe.

He looked up at the painting after reading about it. There were no people, no room and no universe like in the *Star Trek* movies. There were just two very small steel pins with human hands that carried a rolled-up currency note on their heads. It almost made him laugh. But when he saw their shadow, he stopped. The shadow had words written in it, letters really, jumbled up. He tried to connect them, tilting his head to read words like 'pain', 'misery' and 'hate'.

Our thoughts don't come with an expiration date, and that is such a tragedy.

The combination of the words and the white, black and grey paint strokes was disturbing and illuminating at the same time.

Akash pulled himself away for a while. There would be time to see the other paintings later. He was beginning to feel tired. He walked across to the café and ordered a strong cup of coffee, opened his laptop and started to make the necessary changes to his campaign. He changed the telephone number, replacing it with his own, and drafted another press release based on what he saw, what Mr Gaitonde said and the audience's overall reaction.

Mr Gaitonde had also said, 'Subah's work is a searing example of what happens when a human brain observes not from within but from outside the body. These thoughts are pristine and echo a rare sensibility about life around us, the rainbow we mistake for colours and the dark corners we mistake for neglected spaces. Subah is a rare talent.'

He copy-pasted that particular quote everywhere he could. Half an hour later, he closed his laptop and went looking for Mr Taraporewala.

'There you are,' the agent said. 'So, are you happy with the way it's gone so far?'

'Yes, thanks to you.'

'Thanks to Miss Subah. We exist because of talented people like her. You should be proud of working with her.'

Akash considered giving him details but decided against it once again. 'Yes, I am proud. Where is Mr Gaitonde?'

'He had to leave, but he would like to meet Miss Subah whenever she is feeling up to it in the next few days.'

'Thanks, I'll make sure that happens. Subah respects him a lot.'

'Everyone does. By the way, we have sold three pieces today. A good start.'

Akash excused himself to return to the hotel. The hustle and bustle at the venue had diluted his concerns about Subah, but as he walked back to the hotel, he found himself worrying about her once more.

Chapter 39

*B*ack at the hotel, Subah had been worried sick about Bala. She couldn't make an outside call from the phone in her room, so she'd gotten dressed and gone down to the reception desk to call her. But the landline at her home and Bala's mobile both had gone unanswered. She'd finally remembered that one of the criminals who had attacked her had called her home number. How must Bala have reacted? She was very fragile, and even after years of living with Subah, her wounds had not healed properly. Unsure about what to do next, she had sat down in the lobby.

As soon as she saw Akash walk through the swinging doors fifteen minutes later, she was on her feet. 'Akash, do you know where Bala is?'

He filled her in on what had happened and called Rohit to find out the latest. As expected, his friend had been taking due care and was able to inform him that Bala would be discharged later that day, an ambulance dropping her home. After his clinic closed at 9 that night, Rohit's plan was to go and see her.

Akash hung up and informed Subah about the developments while they sat in the lobby. It relaxed her a bit, and after he shared with her the details of the opening and what Mr Gaitonde had said about her work, she felt much better.

'I think I would like to go there tomorrow. Thanks for

everything, Akash. You can return to Delhi now.'

'What are you saying? I've just done my duty, Subah, and I won't be leaving unless I'm sure that you are completely safe and recovered.'

More than the concern and affection, she liked the tone of his voice. He wanted to be in control of the situation, and with him at the helm, she felt her boat was steadier.

'Have you eaten anything since morning?'

She shook her head and replied to his question with a question of her own. 'Have you slept since last night?'

'Well, no. But that's okay. I'm used to it.'

'Used to it?'

'Well...'

'I know.'

'What do you know?'

'Why you are used to *not* sleeping.'

'And why is that?'

'You think a lot about Nisha, and you miss her a lot.'

Akash shuffled his feet, and she watched him closely. His love for his wife had moved something in her. She had never known such intensity of love. Akash's love was different. It was more surreal, almost like an aberration in the world, something that she'd been trying to capture through her works. Her discovery of the connection between her paintings and his love for his departed wife made her feel uncomfortable.

Subah had been in love only once, and it had ended badly. Her friends said there was no such thing as real love and those who carried on saying to each other that they were still in love were simply too weak to step out of a relationship. It was more for convenience than for anything else. Like her mother, who stayed with her father not because she loved him but because she couldn't think of anything else to do.

Akash was different, though. He was the perfect proof that real love was possible.

'I asked you first. Would you like something to eat? I know a place nearby.'

Subah looked into his eyes, and something stirred in the deepest part of her stomach. What should she do? Offer him her hand and walk out those doors like two careless friends or put her arm around him and walk out like lovers?

She was neither a friend nor someone in love with him. How would someone else define their relationship? They were certainly more than just business associates. Because he was here, taking care of her, making sure her event went off well. The extra effort was well outside the boundaries of business. What did he think of her?

The sequence of questions and her answers to them brought her headache back. 'Can we leave in ten minutes?'

'Sure.'

Subah closed her eyes.

After some time, she got to her feet and they left the hotel side by side. They took a left turn outside, and as they rounded a nearby curve, they found themselves in front of the majestic Taj Mahal Palace hotel.

Akash waited for her to enter the revolving doors first before easing himself into the next section, and they soon found themselves in the opulent lobby of the iconic Taj.

On their way there, Subah was aware of their proximity as they walked. As if Akash was making sure that he was in a position to support her if she felt uneasy. For a moment, she wanted to deliberately trip, just to see his reaction. The truth was, she realized, she wanted to be held in his arms once more. And even though it was inappropriate for her to imagine it, she wasn't the least bit angry with herself that she did.

They sat in the Shamiana restaurant on the right side of the lobby.

After they had browsed through the menu for a couple of minutes, Akash asked, 'What would you like to eat?'

'I'm not sure.'

'Are you not hungry?'

'I...'

'Subah, you need to eat to keep up your strength, even if you aren't hungry. What do you like? Indian? Italian? Chinese?'

He finally succeeded in persuading her to make a selection. Subah asked for risotto while Akash settled for fish and chips. And lime soda to drink for both of them.

As they waited for the food to arrive, Subah looked at Akash closely. The man seated before her was a gentleman. In fact, from the moment she had met him, her understanding of men had started to change.

Akash was in love with his wife even after her death. He knew she could never come back, but he was not prepared to contemplate a life without her. As Subah thought more about it, her eyes began to tear up.

'Are you all right?'

'Yes.' After a pause, she continued, 'Tell me what Mr Gaitonde said.'

'What Mr Gaitonde said about your current series was amazing. Mr Taraporewala said that Mr Gaitonde is not known to mince words. He says what he believes.'

'What exactly did he say?' Subah was curious and happy to have the conversation move her away from the unexplained attraction that she felt for Akash.

Akash took out his laptop from his bag, which he'd set down next to his chair, and pressed the start button before speaking. 'I would like to read to you exactly what he said. By the way, I sent it to the media as well.'

After he had read it and briefed her how people were reacting on social media according to the analytics, they turned their attention to the food, which had just arrived. There was no further conversation as they ate silently. Subah's mind had begun to calm down. Akash and the success of her exhibition were pulling her away from the memory of the attack.

After lunch, they walked outside and Subah stared at the sea. It was dusk by then, and she desperately wanted to go to the Gateway of India, just to breathe in the fresh air.

'Let's go there for a while,' Akash said.

'How did you know?' she asked, surprised.

He chose not to answer, and they walked through the same security perimeter she had walked through alone earlier. Once they reached the walls at the end, she watched the boats in awe. Without realizing it, her hand slipped into Akash's, and she only noticed when he gently removed his hand and folded his arms against his chest. She turned to look at him. He was staring back at her, and she couldn't read his expression.

'I'm sorry,' she murmured.

He once again chose not to reply, and yet, it did not make her angry. His presence was comforting.

'Sir, madam, you are such a nice couple, one picture please.' It was a young photographer, who had mistaken them for a couple.

Akash turned away, and Subah did as well. They walked back to the hotel in silence, and as they passed the armed guard, he jumped to attention. When they reached the door to Subah's room, Akash paused and spoke without turning. 'You need to rest. Please take your medicines. I'll see you in the morning.'

She nodded obediently and said, 'And you need to rest too. Thank you and good night, Akash.'

Subah went inside and closed the door. She was alone now, and it wasn't a pleasant feeling. She checked the bathroom, the cupboard and under the bed for any intruders. Not finding any, she sat on the bed and stared at the door.

Chapter 40

When Akash returned to his room, the first thing he did was call his mother. He had spoken to her from the gallery as well, but Sara had still been at school then.

'How's Sara, Mom?'

'She is fine, beta. How's Subah?'

'She's doing okay. Can I speak to Sara?'

He spoke to Sara for a while before hanging up. The voice of his daughter in his ears made him feel a little better.

Akash was tired. But more than that, he was worried. Subah had tried to hold his hand at the Gateway of India. It might have been unintentional, but somewhere at a deeper level, he knew it wasn't. When the photographer had approached the two of them, Akash had been angry but chose to keep his emotions in check.

Now he raised his hand absent-mindedly to examine it and recalled how Subah had described one of her paintings.

Love is not an anchor, it is propulsion, the courage to stem the tide, cut through ocean currents and face the storm together.

Nisha had been his partner to cut through the storms, but she was no longer by his side. Could he fight this battle alone? The answer was *yes*. Because he was not alone; his memories of Nisha helped him fight life's battles every day.

Akash had brought Nisha's final letter with him to Mumbai, and he took it out now to read it.

His wife had wanted him to move on. But he knew that wasn't an option he would ever consider. For him, she was still alive; he could feel her presence in the room even now. With the letter still in his hands, he stretched out on the bed, closed his eyes and exhaled loudly, his thoughts on Nisha.

Akash woke to the ringing of his phone. 'Hello?'

'Akash, Rohit here. I'm calling from Subah's house. Bala is fine, but she wants to speak to Subah.'

'What time is it?'

'What? You sound groggy. Were you sleeping? I'm sorry to have woken you!'

'No, that's okay. I might have dozed off. Yeah, Subah is well, but she's in her room. I'll go ask her to call home. Give me a few minutes.'

'Sure.'

He hung up and looked at the time on his phone. It was 10. He dashed into the bathroom, splashed some cold water on his face and was better oriented when he got back. Next he reached for the intercom.

'Subah, how are you feeling?'

'I'm fine, thank you.'

'Did you take your medicine?'

'Yes, I did, thank you.'

'Why are you thanking me after every answer?'

'What do you mean? It's common courtesy, isn't it?'

'Okay. Can you please call Bala? She's at home now, and Rohit is there too. He went to check on her. She's fine; she just wants to hear your voice.'

'I'll do that, thank you.'

He heard the click in his ear and stared at the phone with a frown before putting it down. What had changed in the last three hours?

Akash turned the kettle on to make some tea, and as the water started to heat, he switched on his laptop. As he waited, he thought more about the day and what lay immediately ahead.

There was a knock. He got up to open the door. It was Subah.

'Hi!' Akash said, surprised.

'Are you all right?'

'Yes, I'm fine.'

'May I come in?'

'Of course.' Akash stepped to one side to let her into his room, then closed the door. By the time he turned, she was already seated in the only chair. He walked across and sat on the bed.

'I don't think I've had the chance to say sorry properly.'

'Sorry about what, Subah?' He knew well what she was about to say but pretended otherwise.

'About the Gateway visit.'

'Oh! Come on. It's okay, Subah. Please don't let that work you up so much. I know you didn't mean it in any inappropriate way.'

'I would like to tell you about my past, if you don't mind.'

'If it makes you feel better, please go ahead.'

'My father and mother have never been in love. They live in the US now, but I was raised here in India because, at that time, they were here. I had a brother too, whom we lost at a young age. Traffic accident.'

'I'm sorry.'

'It broke our family's spirit, but we held on together somehow. Things got better with time, and then I fell in love…' She paused and tried to unlock her throat by swallowing.

Akash handed her a bottle of water.

She took a sip and continued. 'That was the biggest mistake of my life. My boyfriend dumped me for someone else. Just like that. Without any reason.' She took more sips of water, turned her face away from Akash to fight the tears and continued after a minute or so. 'I'd never thought such a thing could happen to me. I thought people separated when they had trouble with each other. That day, I realized that sometimes men just got bored and moved on. My father is one such man. Every time my mother calls, I'm filled with fear. Is she calling to say that Dad has left her?'

Akash opened his mouth to speak but closed it again. Where was she taking him?

'And so I started to help women. Women like me, who have been broken completely, their self-confidence and self-worth killed forever. It gave me strength, and I helped hundreds of such women.'

'I know about your NGO, Subah. And trust me when I say this: Our world is very lucky to have people like you in it.'

Lost in the story she was telling, she didn't seem to hear him. 'I had begun to hate the entire masculine tribe. No exceptions. My mother tried to convince me that I was wrong, but I didn't listen.'

'Well… I think you're—'

'And then I met you. Working with you, I realized that I was wrong. Men are not all the same. You are so different. So, please,

I don't want to lose a good friend because of what happened today. I hope you don't mind if I call you my friend?'

'Of course not. It is a pleasure.'

'Now that I have told you all about me, perhaps you will also be able to forgive me for our very first meeting at the Habitat Centre. I didn't mean to hurt you, it's just that...you're a man, and I got carried away.'

Akash remembered the meeting at the exhibition in Delhi well. In reply, he raised his hand, gesturing that it was okay. After she had stopped speaking, he looked at her. She was a bundle of confidence and nerves all at the same time, like someone who accidently walks into a glass door and smiles without intending to. 'If you don't mind, I'd like you to say more about that man you mentioned.'

She nodded, and her eyes narrowed as she spoke. 'Ours was not a teenage crush kind of a thing. We had had our share of temporary affairs, like everyone else, but when we fell in love with each other, it was real and serious. At least, that's what I thought. He was nice initially... but...he left me for another woman.'

Akash spoke slowly and clearly. 'Why do you say he left you? How about saying he didn't deserve you? That changes everything, doesn't it?'

Even though she had tears in her eyes, Akash noticed a hint of a smile on her face now.

They were quiet for a few minutes before Akash spoke again. 'Did you call Bala?'

'Yes, I did. She's doing fine. Thanks to you and Dr Rohit.'

'Well...we only did our duty.'

'Bala is a beautiful soul.'

'You are a beautiful soul too, Subah. Know that. Respect yourself. That man—'

'I'd like to go now.' She was on her feet. 'Thank you, Akash.'

Before he could say anything, she was gone. He heard the door click and stared at the empty chair for a long time. Finally, around 11, he prepared another cup of tea for himself and ate a few potato crisps. The odd timing of his meal with Subah had thrown off his internal clock, and he wasn't sure which he was more: hungry or sleepy. Finally, he realized that he was neither and switched on the TV to watch a boring movie on mute, hoping to become sleepy. But his mind once again turned to Subah.

Subah was different. Not just in the way she thought, but also in the way she reacted to the world. She was more primal than anyone he had met before, and even though sometimes she seemed as innocent as a child, she was unique and put on no pretences whatsoever. She never boasted about the women she had helped or the accolades she had won. And she was also beautiful in a down-to-earth sort of way. Akash had never seen her make any effort to enhance her looks, yet she still looked beautiful.

As he sipped the tea, his thoughts stayed on Subah.

Her eyes, he had noticed, were clear and intense, and her paintings straight from the heart, matching the appeal of her eyes. In fact, her eyes were the key to her art. They chose the subjects and wrapped an inimitable theme around them as Subah turned them into art. And yet, he now realized that in the two exhibitions he had attended, he had seen only a minimal use of colour. Almost all her works were black and white and the shades of grey in between. As if her eyes could not see any colour.

This was a beautiful, hurt woman, who was trying to keep her sanity intact through art while also working hard to keep as many women safe as possible. And in return, what did she get? Two men attacking her and trying to extract money from her.

If anything, Akash had the deepest respect and admiration for Subah. He was no longer angry with her. Not at the way she had behaved earlier in the evening. Nor for refusing Rohit's advances. Nor for the discourteous way she had treated him during their initial meetings.

As far as Rohit was concerned, maybe she wasn't attracted to him, and what she felt was merely respect. Maybe there was no chemistry, and the sparks Akash had thought he had seen fly at the hospital in Delhi were only in his mind. He started to feel guilty for suggesting that he was angry through his body language at the Gateway. She didn't deserve to be treated in any other way than respectfully.

Akash exhaled loudly, and for the first time, another thought began to take root in his mind. He couldn't deny any longer that he was attracted to her. That had been the case right from the start, only he'd refused to accept it. But why was he thinking differently about her now?

Chapter 41

The trip to Akash's room had pepped up Subah's mood, and she was now looking forward to the next day. She could tell that her relationship with Akash was on an even keel now and they could start afresh. She liked Akash, but more than that, she respected him.

As Johnnie Sparks, he had already spent so much time and money to make her exhibition successful. How would she ever pay him back? She made a mental note to tell him to go ahead and return to Delhi tomorrow and add the extra expenses he'd incurred to what she had initially promised as the fee for his services.

She rechecked the lock of her room, put on the chain lock as an additional measure, turned the bathroom light on before flicking the room lights out, and slipped into bed. She could hear the hum of the air conditioner and nothing else. Her senses heightened, she turned towards the door and looked at the light that seeped from under it. Would she be able to sleep tonight? Last night had been different. Perhaps the drugs given to her intravenously had still been in effect then. But at this moment, she didn't feel sleepy at all.

It turned out to be a long night. Around 2, she heard a sound from outside her door. Her eyes flew open, and she sat upright on the bed, her senses alert once again, eyes unblinking as she focused on the light seeping in from outside. Then she saw the light get darker for just a second, as if someone had passed her door. Who was outside?

Subah started to sweat. There was another sound. Was she hallucinating? Minutes ticked by, but nothing happened. Then there was a knock on the door.

'Who is it?' she asked, her voice uncertain.

There was no answer.

'Who is it?' This time she screamed.

There was still no answer.

At that moment, her phone started to ring. Without taking her eyes off the door, she grabbed it and screamed with all the power in her lungs, 'Who is it?'

'Subah, it's me.'

Akash's voice lessened her hysteria, but her voice still quivered when she spoke. 'Akash, there's someone outside my door. Please help. Help.' She hung up and started laughing. She got up, faced the door and shouted, 'Akash is on his way. Whoever you are, he'll kick your ass.'

After a few seconds, she heard a loud banging on the door and Akash calling her name. She opened it and saw Akash. There was no one else. She grabbed him, pulled him in and locked the door.

He embraced her, and she shivered in his arms for a long time before reality started to soak in again. They were standing close to the bed, and she slowly disengaged herself.

'I'm sorry.' She sat down heavily on the bed. 'I'm not sure what's happening to me.'

Akash sat on the chair and said, 'You don't have to feel sorry.

It's your state of mind due to the PTSD. The hallucinations will lessen over time. It will be okay. You need to fight this, Subah. I'm here to help you however I can.'

'I know about PTSD. I've seen so many women cope with it. Few are able to get through the first, dark phase. Most fail and live with bruises on their soul for the rest of their lives, never normal again, just emotionless bodies of flesh and blood.'

Akash stayed silent, knowing it was best to let Subah talk.

'Knowing something is so different from having to go through it.' After a while, she added, 'I'm sorry. You can go now.'

'Please don't feel guilty. You don't have to be sorry. And I'm not going anywhere. I'll get my mattress and sleep right here on the floor.'

She looked up sharply at him, her eyes searching. This man truly cared like no one else she had met before. Her respect for him rose even higher.

Akash left for a few minutes and returned with his mattress and pillow tucked under his arm. He placed it on the floor beside her bed and looked at her, 'I'm here, and you don't have to worry. Now, try to sleep—we have a long day tomorrow.'

She lay down on the bed, and Akash reached to turn the lights off. The room was dark, but this time, she wasn't scared at all. She wondered again what name she could give to a relationship like this. Nothing came to her mind as she drifted off to sleep.

Chapter 42

The next morning, Akash woke up before Subah. He was groggy for a few seconds, but as he fully woke up to the fact that he was in Subah's room, he was relieved to realize that all was well. Deciding not to disturb her, he prepared a cup of tea for himself and turned to look at her. Just looking at her calm face as she slept was so peaceful that Akash didn't get annoyed with himself when he realized that his tea had turned cold. He brought the cup to his mouth and discovered, for the first time, that cold tea didn't taste all that bad. How long had he been staring at her face?

After he finished his tea, he quietly slipped out and freshened up in his own room. At 9, he was back in Subah's room, only to find that she was still sleeping. The medicine, he thought, and wondered if he should wake her up. He decided not to and parted the curtains to look out the window. From where he stood, he could see cars and people moving soundlessly past restaurants, souvenir shops and designer stores. The pavement was full of people of all ages, hurrying to get to their destinations to start their day. He imagined them calculating prices in their heads as they moved, wondering if it would rain before they reached their journey's end, cursing politicians for the state of affairs and mulling over whether it was the right time to snack on their next vada pav. He allowed the curtain to fall back in place and turned towards the bed.

At that moment, he saw Subah stir and open her eyes. She smiled. He smiled back.

Without asking, he prepared a cup of tea and placed it next to her as she sat up and leant against the headboard. 'How are you feeling today?'

'Reborn.'

'Good enough to visit the gallery?'

'Yes, I want to be near my babies.'

Knowing she was referring to her paintings, Akash smiled. 'That's wonderful. I'll be waiting in my room. Let me know when you're ready, and I'll call a cab.'

'Sure, but let's walk. The exercise will do me good. I don't think it's more than 200 metres anyway.'

He nodded and returned to his room. The fact that she was feeling better had changed the equation between them. From that moment on, he would have to be careful she didn't get the wrong idea. He was there to support her, nothing more. And as soon as he felt she was well enough to take care of herself, he would leave on the first plane.

An hour later, they walked to the gallery. It was around 11, and there weren't many visitors. Mr Taraporewala was there, talking to some people, and as soon as he saw Subah, he beamed and rushed towards her.

'Such a pleasure to see you, Miss Subah. How are you feeling today?'

'Thank you, I'm fine.'

'Hello, Mr Akash.'

'Good morning, Mr Taraporewala.'

'The newspapers have been kind. Have you seen the coverage?'

Akash and Subah exchanged looks. They'd completely forgotten to check the newspapers.

Mr Taraporewala escorted them to one side, where there were many newspapers scattered on a circular table. 'Sorry for the mess. I was trying to cut out the coverage to prepare a folder and send it to your hotel.'

Subah was touched. So was Akash.

Mr Taraporewala started to shuffle through the newspapers. 'Okay, so let me arrange them in some order. Yeah, this here is *DNA*. Here are *The Indian Express* and *Hindustan Times*. Even, surprisingly, *The Times of India*. A few Marathi papers too.'

He placed them in order and invited her to take a look.

Akash looked around for a chair so Subah could sit and read. There was one in the far corner, and he walked across and carried it back. 'Here, sit.'

She looked up from the *DNA* newspaper she was reading, smiled and sat down after thanking him. Akash picked up another paper. The two of them silently consumed the news coverage for the next twenty minutes, as Mr Taraporewala went around helping people who walked in.

Akash was happy. The newspaper coverage was much better than he'd hoped. Most was a mix of what he had shared in the press release and what the reporters had observed during the opening. Mr Gaitonde's remarks were widely reported.

Even though it was to be expected, the fact that more than two-thirds of all the reports focused on the attack on Subah made Akash feel a shade uncomfortable at the increasing commodification of the news. And yet, on the whole, he was happy. At least the people of Mumbai now knew about the exhibition.

He excused himself and moved to another table, where he opened his laptop to check the live updates on social media. Here, too, the results were better than he'd expected. He used his phone to take pictures of the news articles and added them to all the social media extensions he was using in the campaign.

'Thank you, Akash, this is fantastic.' Subah walked towards him, her hands extended. There were tears in her eyes.

He took her hands and hugged her. It was a friendly hug. 'You deserve all the attention, Subah. You're one special person.'

They heard Mr Taraporewala return and disengaged themselves.

Subah hugged Mr Taraporewala.

Akash excused himself again and called home to speak to his mother. Then he called Rohit and explained the events of the previous night in detail.

'This is a typical case of PTSD. You need to be careful, Akash. Many victims of this kind of violence have suicidal tendencies. You did the right thing by staying in her room. I honestly feel she should return here to Delhi. Familiar surroundings will help her recover faster.'

'Let me see if I can convince her to come back. From what little I know of her, she is very stubborn and will not leave her exhibition halfway through.'

'You think I should arrange for Bala to go there? She's feeling better now, and having the two women close to each other will make things a lot easier.'

'That's a good idea. But two problems come to mind. One, the cost, and two, she will be of little use in a strange city. Come to think of it, she most likely will be more of a liability for Subah than any help.'

'Money isn't a major issue. I can take care of it. But I think you're right about the other reason.'

'Hmm.'

'Anyway, let's see how well she copes. Stay close to her, and if you see anything odd, just call a doctor, okay?'

'Sure, thanks.'

'Bye.'

Chapter 43

Subah was overwhelmed by the way Akash had supported and cared for her over the last two days. And he'd had a major role to play in the unprecedented success of her show. By the third evening, half her works had a 'Sold' tag on them.

She had spoken to dozens of buyers, people from the media and many who had identified themselves as activists from the city. Everyone was sorry for the way Mumbai had treated her, and they offered places to stay or cars for her to get about if necessary. Subah was touched by their generosity. One of the schools had sent a few girls and boys with roses. She hugged each of them and cried. An old woman handed her a poem she had written, and Subah was so moved on reading it that she decided to share it with everyone present, but halfway through, her voice choked up. The old woman completed the rest.

Earlier that afternoon, she had accepted an invitation from one of the editors of a popular newspaper to join her for lunch. She had no idea where Akash was at that time. She asked Mr Taraporewala, and he said he didn't know either. She was beginning to understand Akash more now. He was giving her time, perhaps watching her from a distance without her knowing it.

When she arrived at the restaurant for lunch, she ended up

in tears again. Mr Gaitonde was waiting for her. After asking about her health and well-being, he critiqued her paintings in detail and praised her innovative and thoughtful approach. Just being in the company of a master, breathing the same air as him, was perhaps the best moment of her life. She thanked him and the editor profusely after lunch.

Around 6, she saw Akash saunter into the gallery. He smiled at her, and she smiled back. No words were exchanged. None were needed. They walked back to the hotel, took the lift to the third floor and went into their respective rooms.

Upon entering her room, she wrote on the hotel's notepad: *I'm here waiting for you, but I won't really mind if you don't come because I know you want to but can't.*

As she reread it, it gave birth to an image. Without her fully realizing it, her words had become the theme for a painting in her mind. All her works so far had been the products of her imagination, but this one was real. It was about her and Akash. She wished she had a canvas and palette to bring the image to life. After a while, she tore that sheet of paper from the pad, folded it and put it in her pocket.

Though she had spoken to Bala the previous day and given her the hotel's number, she had not spoken to her mom, who must have tried to call her by now. She'd be worried sick at not reaching her. Subah called the reception desk and asked them to connect her to her mother's US number. The receptionist said that it wasn't possible for them to transfer international calls to her room, so she would have to come down to the lobby to make the call.

Subah changed into a shirt and shorts and was in the lobby five minutes later.

'Mom, no, sorry, I'm fine. I've lost my phone. I'll get a new one tomorrow and let you know the number as soon as it's activated. Yes, the exhibition is going fine. More than half of my works are gone. The press has given it extensive coverage.'

This last detail was unnecessary. She bit her tongue and stopped speaking. What if her mother tried to look up the news articles online? She'd learn about the attack on Subah in no time.

Subah decided to wrap up the conversation quickly. 'Mom, I'm doing fine. Here, please take down the hotel's number...' After her mother wrote down the number and read it back to her, Subah said, 'I'll call you from my new number as soon as I have one. Bye. I love you, Mom.'

Subah felt relieved after speaking to her mother and decided to sit in the lobby for a while. There were just two other people there, a man and a woman. Both sat on the same sofa, busily reading the magazines. She took an empty sofa seat and looked outside. The armed guard was still there, and for a brief moment, their eyes met through the doors. She wouldn't have recognized him if he weren't in police uniform—the guards changed with each shift, and she had never seen the same person twice—but his presence made her more comfortable. The Mumbai police had been professional and cooperative with her.

She reached into her pocket and pulled out the card that Santosh Kamble had given her. It had an address and a number on it. She wanted to call him and thank him again. How could she convey her gratitude? Perhaps it wasn't necessary. He was to her what she had been for so many women. And just like she didn't expect the women to thank her again and again, neither would he. She was certain of it, and yet, she felt so grateful to him.

It had also been three days since she had spoken to Prerna

and Aparna, her new staff at the Jor Bagh office of Help Forever. She called them from the reception desk and was relieved to hear that there had been no noteworthy developments. She gave them the hotel's number too.

By then, it was around 8 and she was hungry. Where was Akash? Had he even eaten lunch?

Chapter 44

*A*kash had deliberately stayed away from Subah that day. She was in a safe place and surrounded by admirers and the media.

In the afternoon, he had seen her leave the gallery with an editor he had met earlier and kept his distance. And after the gallery closed for the evening, he had walked with her wordlessly to the hotel. Somehow, there seemed to be no need to speak.

Sleeping in her room last night had completely wiped out the wedge he'd felt between them. Subah was a beautiful soul, and she deserved a great day like today after what she'd gone through.

While at the gallery, Akash had used the time to post more information on social media. He had taken a few pictures of Subah talking to people and added them too. These were the first images of the artist at her exhibition, and he was sure that they would add the necessary impetus to the overall campaign. He had also bought a simple phone for Subah, using a copy of her ID to reapply for her old number, and was relieved to be assured that the number would be activated within a day.

As he took a shower in his hotel room, he thought about what Rohit had said. Since he had no job commitments waiting for him in Delhi and the only one he had been partly paid for was still a few weeks away, Akash had time on his hands. That meant he could stay in Mumbai for a few more days to watch over Subah and her exhibition.

But he missed Sara terribly. The first thing he did after leaving the bathroom and getting dressed was call her.

'Dad, how is the painter aunty now?'

'Hey, how did you know?'

'Dadi told me yesterday.'

'She's fine.'

'Is she with you now? Can I talk to her?'

'No, she is not here; she is in her room.'

'Her room? But why are you not in the same room?'

'Okay, no more about that. Tell me, how was school today?' he asked, changing the subject, and was relieved when Sara told him stories about her friends. This conversation was between father and daughter, and he didn't want too much mention of Subah in it.

When Subah didn't answer the phone fifteen minutes later, Akash called the reception desk, trying to keep his worries in check.

'Sir, madam is here in the lobby. You want me to call her?'

'No, I'm coming down.' Akash was down in a few minutes.

'Hi, Akash. Looks like you're out to impress someone. Fresh and ready.'

'Thanks.' He didn't know how to react to such a comment. He wasn't prepared for such frankness from her. But it was a good sign. Subah was almost back to her normal self, and that was what mattered at the moment. 'There might be someone,' he played along, winking.

'If you don't mind, can I come along and see who this person is? I just have to go to my room to change. Won't take longer than fifteen minutes.'

'Sure, I'll wait here.'

Half an hour later, Subah was back down, and for the first time, the way she looked took his breath away, making him speechless. She wore a knee-length yellow dress with big flowers on it, a pearl necklace and heels. Her face glowed. Subah the painter, the saviour of women, looked stunning.

'Let's find out who this person is that you're trying to impress.'

All he could do was nod, and the two of them walked from their hotel towards the PJ Ramchandani Marg, which joined the Gateway of India to the Radio Club.

'Where were you today, Akash?'

'I was doing some work. You know the—'

'Did you eat lunch?'

'Yes, I did.'

'Where?'

'Well, there was this place—'

'I know you didn't, so please don't lie to me.'

Akash didn't say anything. Even though her comments had some overtones of ownership, he wasn't annoyed. They were good friends now, and she was entitled to it. She was right, he had not eaten lunch. But he had had lots of tea and biscuits, so he hadn't even realized that he'd missed a meal.

They passed people, mostly tourists, Arab men and women in their traditional clothes, sailors from the nearby harbour with their crew cuts and the local Mumbaikars with smiles on their faces. They walked past a Starbucks and a few Iranian cafés before turning left.

'Oh, by the way, here is your new phone. Your previous number should be activated soon. Just keep it charged and switched on.'

'Thank you.'

'You're welcome.'

'Where exactly are we going?'

'I'm not sure. Do you have a place in mind?'

'No.'

A diner appeared on their right, and Akash looked at Subah. She nodded, and they entered. It was a small place with few occupied tables. They chose a table by the window that overlooked the road outside.

'What's special here?' Akash asked the waiter, who appeared by their side as soon as they were seated.

'Seafood, sir.'

'Would you like that?' he asked Subah.

'Yes, very much. What about you?'

'Yeah, me too.'

'Indian or Chinese? I'm afraid they don't have Italian, your favourite.'

'I love Indian too.'

Akash asked the waiter for fish and prawns with rotis and a biryani, then asked Subah, 'Would you like to have a beer? Or wine maybe?'

'I would prefer beer, but we can do wine if you like.'

Akash asked the waiter for two pints of beer.

Chapter 45

*S*ubah thought about the only man she had ever loved. That man had touched her body many times but never her soul.

At that time, she hadn't known what love really meant, and after he had ditched her, she had rejected the whole idea of love between man and woman altogether. And seeing her father ill-treat her mother all these years kept her wounds fresh.

But it was different now. All her ideas and beliefs had been altered by the man seated opposite her at the diner. She recalled the way he had held her during the night and thought: *The best surprise is when someone you think will speak to you conveys the message not through words but by touching you.*

In the last three days, their need to communicate through words had lessened. Now she knew why people who cared for each other communicated better by holding hands and finding answers in each other's eyes.

But were they friends or lovers? And what was the difference between the two?

Friendship is the marriage of two minds, whereas love is the marriage of two souls.

The thought left her wondering how accurate this streak of imagination was. Perhaps this thought was perfect for a painting too. The tragedy was that, in her life, she had experienced neither friendship nor love. Now at least she knew what friendship was.

'Akash, you will be my friend for the rest of my life, won't you?'

'Of course I will.'

Subah had the elusive feeling that Akash was attracted to her. She could see it in the way he looked at her. But that was the limit of their relationship, and even though she wanted to be held in his arms—not as a broken person but as someone in love—she knew it wasn't possible.

It started to rain, and she looked outside, her mood lifting. 'Akash, would you like to get wet in the rain?'

'No, I've just had a bath.'

'A good bath can make you feel alive, but if you really want to talk to your body, try dancing in the rain.' She saw him hesitate. 'Come on!'

She put her beer bottle down and was out the door before he could react. Subah was drenched within seconds, and she looked at Akash from outside, making faces, teasing him. The rain felt good on her skin. When Akash came outside too, she was surprised and ran towards him. It had been her shooting-star-make-a-wish moment, and it had worked.

He extended his hands, and she took them gleefully, wondering what he was up to. There was a song playing nearby, and they did a little impromptu dance. Their steps didn't match, but their moods were in sync, so it didn't matter. The song was over in just a minute, and Subah cursed it for being so short. Akash shook his head, playfully directing the droplets in her direction. She jumped in the puddle around her feet to pay back the prank and laughed as he stepped away.

Five minutes later, when they were settled on their seats again after a visit to the restroom to dry off, Subah wondered about her behaviour. She had behaved like a teenager, and yet there was no feeling of regret.

'That was fun, Subah. Thanks! I love your spontaneity. This is life. Life is to be lived.'

Somewhere in the deepest part of her heart, she felt like Akash had changed in those five minutes. The way he looked at her made her conscious of how she looked. As she shifted to banish the thought, their legs touched under the table, and she felt something stir in her stomach.

'Thanks.' That was all she could say as the food was served.

Later, when they walked back to the hotel, she shivered. The temperature had dropped due to the rain, and when they were hit by a sudden gust of wind as they turned towards their hotel, she instinctively moved closer to him. She felt him take her hand, and she let him. For the final hundred metres, they walked holding hands. Anyone watching them would have thought of them as lovers.

'Would you like a cup of coffee?' asked Akash when they reached the third floor.

'I would love one. But can I join you in a few minutes?'

'Sure.'

Subah unlocked her door and went inside.

What was happening?

Why was Akash changing the equation between the two of them? This wasn't right.

Not for him, not for her, not for little Sara.

And most of all, not for Nisha, with whom he was still in love.

Her first thought was to call him and say that she was tired. But something within her resisted. Part of her wanted to go back and spend more time with him. After a minute of internal dilly-dallying, that part won, and she found herself changing into a fresh dress.

Chapter 46

*A*kash was confused. He wasn't sure he'd done the right thing. Perhaps he had taken Rohit's advice too seriously. Perhaps he had allowed himself to be controlled by his primal instincts. Perhaps it was something else. Whatever the case, he was getting into dangerous territory. Subah was a beautiful woman, and he knew that from now on, he would have to be more careful. Just do enough to make her continue to feel taken care of, nothing more.

For the first time, he was not in full control of his emotions. He thought about Nisha, and that brought him closer to reality. He had a wife he was in love with, even though she was no longer in the world. And he had a daughter to take care of. The woman in the next room, however attracted he felt, was just his client, and he was only trying to protect her.

There was a light knock on the door. Akash took a deep breath and opened it. 'Hi again.' She walked past him, and even before she could sit down, he asked, 'What will you have?'

'Wine, if possible.'

'Oh, I meant coffee or tea.'

'Tea is fine, thank you.'

'If you want wine, I have a bottle of that too.' *Why did you have to say that?* he admonished himself, but the bullet had been fired.

'Which kind? If it's red, I'm good.'

He opened the fridge and pulled out the bottle of red wine. There was no white wine, and he secretly wished she had asked for white. It was a screw-top bottle, so he could open it easily, but at that moment, he realized that there were no wine glasses in the room.

He cursed silently and reached for the phone to ask for some to be sent up. They waited, both wondering what to say.

Subah broke the silence. 'People talk when they want to impress, but they smile only when they mean it.'

'Yeah, makes sense.'

'I like your smile, Akash.'

'And I like the way you smile with your eyes, Subah. Because I know that eyes that have cried a lot only know how to smile and talk. Not everyone can smile with their eyes.'

'Thanks, Akash. I didn't know you were a poet.'

'When a person speaks heartfelt truth, it becomes poetry.'

There was a knock on the door. The wine glasses had arrived.

Akash poured the wine into both glasses and handed one to Subah. 'Cheers to the success of your show.'

'Cheers to you for being the strongest pillar in making it successful.'

Akash took a sip and said, 'The idea of getting wet in the rain was a good one.'

'I love the rain, and thanks for the dance. I felt like a human being for the first time in a long time.'

'I loved dancing too. It was spontaneous. I didn't know what was happening, but I loved it.'

They were quiet again. The time was around midnight, and the wine bottle was almost empty. Considering that the two of them had had beer earlier, it was way too much alcohol for one day for Akash, and surely for Subah as well, he thought. But somehow, the mood, the weather and the headiness of the success of the day all combined to make him feel light in the head, not drunk.

'I think I should be going now, Akash.' Subah got to her feet and started to move towards the door. As she bent down to place her wine glass next to where Akash was seated, her hand brushed his shoulder.

Akash felt his face turn hot. Her hand was still extended, and he took it and turned her towards him.

What am I doing? The part of him asking that question was too small and weak.

Subah looked into his eyes and spoke slowly. 'The eyes speak the language of the heart. You can fool people by speaking through your mouth, but eyes, Akash, eyes don't lie. And therefore, I know what you're thinking.'

After that, she closed her eyes.

Akash hesitated. He was not completely in control of himself. Or maybe he was.

Her lips were full, and when she opened her eyes again after a few seconds, he felt like he was standing on a beach and the waves were sucking the sand out from under his feet. He felt a tremor, as if he would lose his balance and fall. One moment she was a simple girl, but so close up, she had transformed into something very different. Something that was playing with the chemical balance in his brain.

He bent down and gently placed his lips on hers. He felt her warmth and her trembling. He moved ever so slightly and smelt her breath. As his kiss became more passionate, he felt her mouth open and was possessed by an enormous desire to make love to her. His tongue rushed inside, and his hands began to move over her back as he held her close. His hands seemed to be protesting the dress she was wearing, gently tugging and pulling at it. It was at that moment that she pushed him away.

'No, Akash, this is wrong.'

'I'm sorry.'

With that, she was gone. Akash sat down heavily on the bed. His mind was still buzzing, and it took him some time to get the sequence of events right. He wasn't proud of what had happened just now. His first reaction was to blame the alcohol. He shouldn't have drunk so much. In addition, he shouldn't have called her to his room after dinner.

What have I done? Shit.

He repeated this again and again.

How would he face Subah now? She might think that this had been his intention right from the start. That was how men were, according to her—always conniving, with everything having to end up in a bed. And he had done exactly that. If there was one outcome in the world he had not expected from his Mumbai trip, it was this—his kissing another woman.

Was there any more wine left? He found another bottle in the fridge, opened it and drank straight from the bottle. He was not just angry with himself but with Subah too.

Grey can have fifty shades, never more, but love has a million.

The thought made perfect sense. The world that Subah inhabited was all grey, but he was in love with Nisha and his life was not all grey. He was richer than her by a million shades.

He drank some more and soon started to feel drowsy. Placing the bottle on the floor, he got into bed. He needed to think. Without knowing it, Akash was asleep in no time.

Chapter 47

*S*ubah wasn't angry. She just didn't know what to think. For a change, even her inner voice was silent. She sat down on the bed, her face resting on her palms, elbows on her knees. Her hair fell forward and covered her face and hands.

In the last few minutes, everything had changed. Not just the equation between the two of them but also what she wanted from life. She closed her eyes, beginning to wonder if all this was her fault. Nothing was clear any more.

Subah got up and looked into the mirror. Her skin was flushed, and she still felt weak in the knees.

A man had kissed her, and she hadn't resisted. That was the simple fact.

It made her feel guilty. She had cheated herself, refused to learn from her past experience and done something she always preached to others not to. What did that make her? A hypocrite? She needed to talk to someone. She needed to clear her head and find her sanity again.

Subah looked hard in the mirror and said, 'Inner voice, why are you silent now? Come on, help me out, will you?'

But nothing happened. Perhaps her inner voice had merged with her because, without her knowing it, this was the direction she'd been guided in all along.

There was another fact she could no longer turn away from. That she'd secretly wanted Akash to kiss her. But when he did, she was scared. Scared of the fact that perhaps Akash wasn't ready for this. She could have gone the distance, but she hadn't wanted it to happen like an accident. She would wait, and if they were destined to be together, it would happen under better circumstances and with clearer intentions.

Go the distance. I know what you mean by that. Her inner voice had returned.

Subah shot back. 'How very convenient. You're not worried about me. Where were you this last half-hour? Tell me, huh, where were you?'

She stared at her reflection and watched her lips curl into a smile. Then the image in the mirror laughed.

'Stop laughing and please tell me what's happening. What's your agenda?'

Goodbye, Subah. I want you to be happy. That's my only agenda. Because I'm you. Just you.

Subah moved away from the mirror and, this time, sat in the chair. After a while, her heartbeat returned to normal, and she changed her clothes and switched off the lights. Then she thought about her day.

It was almost like a dream. A wonderful day, with so much appreciation for her work, not just from the press and art lovers but also from the master himself. She was confident that all her works would find good homes in the next couple of days. And now this. She could still smell Akash's breath on her and feel his hands on her body.

Today, she wasn't scared of anything or anyone in the world. She had someone who cared for her right in the next room. She had always believed her mother when she had said that good things happened to good people … until her heartbreak. But now, her mother's words came back to her.

'Thank you, Mom. Now I know that you were right. Good things really do happen to good people,' she whispered in the darkness.

The room was completely dark. Today, she didn't need the bathroom light on. Today, she didn't turn towards the door to watch the light seeping through. She just closed her eyes, hoping for reality to merge with her dreams.

The next morning, she ate breakfast in her room and was ready by 9. What was Akash doing? How had he taken what had happened between them? Did it upset him? Was he mad at her?

She called him on the phone and didn't get a reply. Just then, there was a knock on the door. Room service was there to clear the breakfast tray. Before closing the door, the man reached into his pocket and pulled out a folded piece of paper.

'Madam, this is from Akash sir.'

What was this?

Why a letter?

Her heart began to flutter, and she thought about poetry. She opened the letter and began to read.

Dear Subah,

I'm sorry, I had to leave suddenly. It's on account of work. One of my client's events has been moved up a couple of weeks, and there's a lot to be done. He wants to meet in person, and we need to finalize a few important things.

I enjoyed your company in Mumbai, and I'm happy that the exhibition is doing better than either of us had hoped. Don't worry,

I'll keep a close watch from Delhi and will do everything possible to publicize it as much as the Internet allows. If you need anything, remember, I'm just a phone call away.

Warmly,

Akash

Is that it? she thought. *I enjoyed your company. That's it?*

Had the evening meant nothing more to him?

She tore the letter in as many parts as she could and threw them in the dustbin.

'Enjoyed your company,' she muttered. After some time, she began to wake up to the facts. She was being unreasonable. For Akash, as for her, work was really important. She had never seen him take his professional commitments lightly. And if there had been a change in schedule, any professional would do the same thing. But why hadn't he spoken to her in person to explain the situation? Perhaps he'd had to leave in the middle of the night, or maybe early in the morning, and hadn't wanted to disturb her. In any case, she would be back in Delhi herself in three more days.

Her anger subsided, but her mood remained sombre. The idea of going to the gallery suddenly seemed less exciting.

Her phone rang. She was glad that her number had finally been activated, but since she'd lost her entire contact list, she had no idea who was calling. 'Hello?'

'Madam, good morning. How are you feeling today?'

'Good morning, Mr Taraporewala,' she said, recognizing his voice. 'I'm okay, thank you.'

'You will feel really wonderful when you see today's newspapers. You're in almost all the papers. This is unprecedented.

I can't remember any exhibition, except a few by top international painters, that was covered back to back for two successive days.'

'All thanks to you.'

'You are welcome. But I think the real credit goes to your work. And, of course, to your employee, Akash.'

'He is not my employee. He is—'

'He isn't? But when I addressed him as an employee, he never objected. So who is he?'

'Well, he is...he is helping me promote my event.'

'Oh. I like him. So, what time shall I expect you here? There are a couple of people already waiting to meet you.'

'I'm not sure.'

'What? Are you unwell?'

'No, I'm fine. I'll try to be there as soon as I can. Thank you, Mr Taraporewala.'

She hung up. Mr Taraporewala had been treating Akash like her employee all this time, and Akash hadn't reacted to it. That was Akash for you: humble, helpful, professional and down to earth. Her anger subsided some more. Perhaps she shouldn't read too much into his sudden departure. She needed to be practical and not a bundle of nerves. She wanted to get back into her old skin; she wanted to be the woman she was before she arrived in Mumbai.

Subah looked into the mirror, smiled reassuringly, picked up her phone and purse, and was soon walking towards the gallery, her head held high.

Chapter 48

*A*kash had lied to Subah. He had woken up at 4 that morning, sweating, feeling guiltier than before. The effects of the alcohol had dissipated, and he couldn't bear the thought of what had happened between him and Subah. He was still in the same room where he had kissed another woman and cheated on Nisha. The room began to suffocate him.

Wondering what he should do next, Akash took a cold shower. The water stung his skin, but he didn't shiver, just kept his head down, watching the water run down the drain. Ten minutes later, when he stood before the mirror, he knew what to do.

He packed quickly and called a cab. On the way, he checked the flight status and booked the earliest flight to Delhi. He wanted to return home, to the world of Sara and his mother, closer to memories of Nisha.

When the flight took off at 7, the city of Mumbai was just waking up. He stretched his neck to look out the window and thought about the note he'd left for Subah with the receptionist. How would she react? That was none of his business. His business with her was almost over, and now all he needed to do was monitor her exhibition. He had already over delivered, so there should be no guilt. The memory of the kiss still bothered him, but he knew that if he kept his distance from her in the future, it would fade too.

He got home at 10, and Sara was still at school.

'How was your trip, beta?'

'It was nice, Ma.' He removed his shoulder bag and sat down on the sofa. He knew what would come next and began to think of the best ways to distract her. 'Ma, is there any breakfast left?'

'I'll make some fresh for you. What would you like?'

'Anything.' He took out his laptop from his bag and switched it on to indicate to his mother that she should leave him alone.

'How about aloo parathas? And tea?'

'Great,' he said without looking up.

As soon as his mom had left for the kitchen, he breathed easier. His phone buzzed. It was a text from Subah. *Thanks for all you've done, Akash. Best wishes, Subah.*

He almost cried in relief. She had taken the cue and was as formal in her text as he had been in his letter. That was nice. He decided not to answer it.

Later, as he sat at the dining table, eating, his mother in the opposite chair, he knew there would be no escape now.

'How is Subah?'

'Oh, Subah's fine. Her exhibition is doing great.'

'How can she be fine? I read about what had happened in the newspaper. I don't think she can be normal for a long time. Who is there taking care of her?'

'Ma, I don't know. To me, she appeared to be fine.'

'Son, look here. What are you hiding from me?'

'Hiding? What's there to hide, Ma?'

'Then why are you not looking at me? Why has your voice changed? Look at your hands. Why are you trembling?'

Akash pushed his chair back and walked away. The way his

mother put it filled him with guilt again. He could speak any number of lies to his mother now or to Subah in the letter, but in his heart, he knew that he had chosen to leave her alone in Mumbai. In short, he had abandoned her.

What was her fault? Nothing.

What was his fault? Everything.

Akash put his hands to his temples and pressed hard. Then, slowly, he looked up at the picture of Nisha.

'I'm sorry, Nisha.'

Chapter 49

*A*kash's mother heard the word 'sorry' and turned back from the door. She had followed her son to the bedroom and was about to say something when she heard it. It was a private moment and she didn't want to intrude. Laxmi left the bedroom, careful not to make any sound, and returned to the living room.

She was confounded. Her son was not telling her the truth. Something had happened in Mumbai, and she didn't have a good feeling about it. She decided to give it some more time and, in order to distance herself from the moment, started to prepare lunch.

When Sara returned from school, she cried with joy upon seeing Akash. 'Dad!'

'I love you, Sara.' He picked her up and kissed her.

'I love you too, Dad. Where is Subah Aunty?'

'She is in Mumbai.'

'Dadi said she was injured. How is she now?'

'She's fine. But tell me, how was your day at school?'

'I want to eat pizza, Dad. Dadi didn't order pizza while you were gone.'

'We will all eat pizza for dinner tonight.'

'Yay!' she shouted and signalled that she wanted to get down. Akash put her down, and she ran inside.

After lunch, Akash called Rohit and told him he was back.

'Back? Why? When? You should have stayed there, Akash. I told you, she's very vulnerable all alone there.'

'I know, but one of my clients wanted me here. An event has been rescheduled.'

'Okay, but...I don't know. You should have made some arrangement.'

'She's 100 per cent normal, Rohit.'

'She can't be. Her trauma is just three days old. What you saw was a temporary good feeling, perhaps due to the success of the show you were telling me about.'

There were other reasons too, all my doing, Akash thought.

Had she really been feeling better because she was under the impression that a romance was blossoming between them? The events in Mumbai once again played out in his mind. Did he overreact? He could have just allowed her to continue with that idea and spent a few more days with her. As if it were some kind of therapy. Even as he was thinking that, part of him knew that these were just excuses, that all he wanted was to go back to her. He was surprised by this train of thought. He was even more surprised that he was no longer irritated with her.

'Are you there?'

'Sorry, I got distracted. What were you saying?'

'Never mind the details now. I think you should have stayed in Mumbai, Akash.'

'Yeah, you're right, Rohit. Perhaps.'

Chapter 50

For Subah, the next three days passed like some kind of dream. Her world was dull without Akash by her side, but she knew that everything else that was happening to her was good. All her works had been sold, and there was nothing left for her to pack and take back.

One day before her exhibition was to conclude and after they had sold the last of her works, Mr Taraporewala invited her to his brother's café for Irani chai. While he was ordering, Subah added that she would like to have her chai with bun-maska. He nodded, a hint of a smile on his face.

'Okay, so we have one day remaining, but there's nothing left for us to show. What would you like me to do?'

Subah had anticipated this and spoken to the management during the lunch break, making a proposal that had brought smiles to their faces. It was time for her to put her plan into action.

'Last evening, I went for a stroll in the Flora Fountain, Churchgate and CST station areas. I've selected five artists—three young men and two women—who were selling their art on the street. All in their early twenties, except for one woman, who seemed to be in her sixties.' The tea was served, and she continued after they had taken their first sips. 'They will exhibit their works in my hall. Let them keep all the money they make. Management has already given their approval.'

Mr Taraporewala smiled, and she was surprised to see how it lit up his face. She hadn't seen him smile like that before. 'That's really good, really good.'

'Thank you! And you look so good when you smile, Mr Taraporewala. Why don't you smile more often?'

His smile faded a bit as he said, 'It's a long story, Subah Madam. I'll share it with you some day. But seriously, thank you, this is the best gift you could have given to the city of Mumbai.'

'Thank you.'

'You know, there are many artists in our world, but very few like you, who know how to keep art alive by contributing meaningfully.'

They finished the bun-maska, and before departing, she said, 'Mr Taraporewala, I'll be leaving tonight. Thank you for all your help. You're a gem.'

'I'm an ordinary person. You are a gem who sees everyone else as a gem. Goodbye, Subah Madam. I hope to see you again soon.'

Subah had not changed rooms after Akash left. She slept alone, the memory of the last evening with Akash keeping her sanity intact. Akash hadn't called, but he had sent her a couple of emails saying that the campaign was doing well.

Subah returned to Delhi on the evening of the same day she had bid farewell to Mr Taraporewala. Upon her arrival, she took a cab straight home from the airport.

Bala opened the door and said, 'Subah, it's so good to see you.'

The two women embraced in her home in Vasant Kunj. After

chatting with Bala for a while, she climbed the stairs to check out her studio. When she switched the lights on, her world came alive: unfinished paintings, unsold paintings, raw ideas on canvas, paint brushes, palettes, paints, stands, varnish bottles, stained towels, water cups and sketchbooks.

Subah was home. In her city.

Also the city where Akash lived. In reality, she knew, there wasn't any 'happily ever after' for them. But reality was no longer a burden, now that she had a memory to cling to.

Chapter 51

*A*s soon as Sara left for school, Akash went to a park near his house. It was an early summer day, and the park was full of people. The sun shone in the dew on the grass, and the flowers were bright, colourful and numerous.

After walking along the jogging track for some time, he sat on a bench and thought about his world. He had everything under control. Last night, just as Sara had requested, they had eaten pizza and he had read a story to her in bed. His business alter ego, Johnnie Sparks, was doing well too.

All that remained of the Mumbai incident was just the dull throb of a memory that he was confident of dislodging from his subconscious in time. His thoughts turned towards Nisha. It was during times like these that he missed her the most. He imagined her sitting beside him, and it brought a smile to his face.

It was at that moment that he realized he had not read Nisha's letter the previous night. It was something he had never done before. Akash began to sweat. He got up and started walking. After a bit, he started to run, trying in vain to outrun himself. Half an hour later, tired, profusely sweating and out of breath, he stopped.

Why had he not read Nisha's letter?

As he regained his senses ten minutes later, he realized the reason.

He had forgotten.

The thought upset him. He closed his eyes, angry with himself. *This can't be happening*, he thought. The tide of the present was so high that he could no longer turn back and see the calm seas of the wonderful times gone by. His present seemed to have consumed his past.

Then he realized that he had not read Nisha's letter on his last night in Mumbai either. That was another blow.

Something surely was changing him from the inside without his knowledge.

After returning home, he watched his mother cook in the kitchen. She worked too hard to support him when it should have been the other way around. His illusion of being in control took another hit.

'Mom, please don't cook dinner tonight. It's my turn.'

She glanced at him, wiped the sweat from her forehead with a towel, and smiled. 'Son, please let me. It's no trouble at all. I love taking care of you and Sara. Who else is there for me to worry about?'

Akash shrugged and decided to immerse himself in work. But the words on the laptop screen made no sense to him. He felt a lack of energy around him and found it difficult to focus on what he was trying to do. After half an hour, he shut down his laptop and stared at the wall. He was lonely, disoriented and confused.

An hour later, Akash left home. It was Rohit's day off, so they'd decided to meet for lunch. Rohit had suggested a new place in Khan Market this time. Besides Rohit, Akash and James, there was Varun, who Akash had met a couple of times before. They started with beer right away.

'So, tell us about Mumbai, Akash,' Rohit asked just as they were finishing their first round of beer and snacks.

'It was good. My client had a major success,' Akash answered for everyone's benefit.

'Is Subah back in Delhi now?'

'I'm not sure.' This time, he answered only to Rohit.

'Why? Haven't you spoken with her?'

'Hey, who's Subah?' It was Varun, dragging the conversation back to the whole table.

'Well, she's—'

'They won't tell you, so don't bother.' That was James.

'Subah is Akash's client and friend, okay?' said Rohit.

The conversation veered in another direction as James mentioned the ongoing 20-20 cricket series. Akash was relieved. He didn't want to take part in any discussion about Subah and be reminded of his last evening in Mumbai.

An hour later, Varun was the first to leave, as he had to get back to work. James excused himself a little later and went on his way too. Akash and Rohit were left alone. They had finished their beer, eaten a hearty lunch and shared some dessert too. Akash was feeling slightly tipsy, and that relaxed him a bit.

'By the way, Akash, I had a chat with Subah this morning. She told me all about Mumbai.'

Akash sat up straighter and eyed him suspiciously. 'What do you mean, all about Mumbai?'

'Well, the exhibition, its success, the press coverage, sales and how you two enjoyed each other's company. I'm a doctor, so I needed to know everything, even the smallest detail.'

'Look, it wasn't planned.'

'Of course. Nothing can be planned 100 per cent.'

'I had to leave Mumbai because of work.'

'That's a lie.'

'What?'

'I've known you forever, Akash. Please don't lie to me.'

'Okay, it is a lie. But what did you expect me to do?'

'You should have stayed.'

'Not after that... She told you about it, didn't she?'

'Well...' Rohit let it linger, looking at Akash with renewed interest.

'It was an accident.'

Even though he had no idea what Akash was talking about, Rohit started to get the drift and a plan began to emerge in his mind. 'You like her, don't you?'

'Are you crazy?'

'We can talk about something else, Akash, if this hurts.'

'You like her too. So what?'

'Look into my eyes and tell me you don't like her.'

Akash raised his head and said nothing.

Chapter 52

*L*axmi opened the door the next day and found Rohit standing there.

'Namaste, Aunty. How are you?'

'Namaste, beta. I'm fine. Please come in.'

He walked in and looked around. 'Where's Akash?'

'He's just gone to the grocery store around the corner. Should be back in ten minutes. Would you like a cup of tea?'

'No, please don't bother. I've just had tea. I'll wait for him.' Rohit sat down. So did Laxmi.

It was Laxmi who spoke first. 'Tell me about Subah.'

They chatted for half an hour, and both were glad that the conversation took place. After Rohit shared what had happened at their last lunch party and Laxmi updated him on Akash's weird behaviour since he had got back from Mumbai and the fact that he felt he had to apologize to Nisha, both were in a better position to understand the situation.

'Aunty, well, I think Akash likes Subah, and something tells me she likes him too. The fact that she recovered so fast in Mumbai after he went there points towards that. I've been speaking to him every day, and as his best friend, I see more than others can. In many ways, he's transparent to me.'

'He has always been poor at hiding his emotions.' She asked

the most important question, which had been bothering her. 'But, beta, you like Subah too, don't you?'

He looked up sharply and said, 'I did. But not any longer. I think Subah is more like Akash. She can't hide what she's feeling either. Just like him, she is passionate, a bit crazy...' He laughed, Laxmi joining him, before continuing, '...in a good sense, of course. And just like Akash, she doesn't play games. I think I'll be happy to just be friends with her.'

'I'm like a mother to you, Rohit—'

He cut her short. 'And therefore you can see that I'm speaking the truth.'

The door opened, and Akash walked in.

'Hey.' Rohit got up, and they hugged and backslapped each other. Akash handed over the bag of groceries to his mother, and the men sat side by side on the sofa.

Rohit left an hour later. By then, Sara had returned from school, and as soon as he left, they sat down to eat lunch. Akash had asked Rohit to join them, but he had said he had to be somewhere else.

After lunch, while Sara watched her favourite cartoon on the TV in the bedroom, Akash's mother came and sat on a chair opposite where he was working at the dining table, his laptop open before him.

The truth was, Akash wasn't working, but just pretending that he was. He was still grappling with the questions of the morning. The whys, ifs and buts had, over time, multiplied, and he was no longer sure if he was closer to the truth or further away from it. He knew he had to make a very important decision about his life but wondered what that decision was.

'Akash?'

He looked at his mother. Her face was tilted at an odd angle, the eyes distant, her mouth twitching. All these years, his mother had read his mind and known what he was about to say. But today, for the first time, he had an idea what was on *her* mind. Did that mean he had crossed a crucial threshold in his life, something that had renewed his understanding of human relationships?

But what his mother had in mind was precisely what he didn't want to discuss.

He got up and moved to the balcony. It was an unusually hot afternoon, and the sun was high in the sky. There were no clouds, and the entire balcony was bathed in white light. But Akash didn't mind. His only objective was to stay away from the thoughts about Subah that crowded his mind wherever he went. Now even his mother was on the verge of broaching the topic.

What was he afraid of? He just had to say *no,* and he knew that after some persistence, everyone would give up. But that was exactly the problem. He wasn't sure how he would react. Would he really say *no?*

Had he fallen in love with Subah? He was no longer certain, but he was sure of one thing—if he agreed with what Nisha had meant in the letter when she said *move on,* it had to be towards a future with Subah.

Strangely, he did want to *move on,* but he didn't want to let go of the past.

'Son, I need to speak to you.' His mother was standing next to him on the balcony now.

Akash nodded and stepped into the living room. He was prepared to face the harshness of the weather, but he was not prepared to subject his mother to it.

They settled on the sofa.

'Beta, I want to talk to you about something very important.'

'Sure, Mom.'

'I want you to allow Subah to take Nisha's place.'

He got to his feet. 'What are you saying, Ma?'

'Sit down.' It was difficult for Akash to make out if that was an order or a suggestion.

He sat down.

Chapter 53

'Akash, I'm your mother. I know you, perhaps, as well as you know yourself, if not better.'

'Ma, please. Let's not discuss it. I already feel so drained by what's happening to me.'

'All I'm asking is that you hear me out, please.'

He looked up.

His mother continued, 'Yes, just listen to what I have to say. And after that, do whatever makes you happy. I won't disagree with you. In fact, let me tell you now, I'll welcome your decision. You are my only son. To me, nothing is more important than your happiness.'

Akash said nothing.

'You know that, when I went to Haridwar for the first time after your father passed away, I stayed for two weeks in an ashram. During that time, I didn't speak to anyone, didn't respond to anyone's greetings and didn't fold my hands during the arti. I was bitter. Everything felt wrong. But slowly, over time, I started to see beauty in the small things. I started to feel pain. I started to imagine a future with you and Sara. What had changed? My surroundings were the same. The thing that had changed was *me*. I'd decided to forget the sorrow and move on. One day, I met a priest who said it's all karma. Our happiness and pain is our own doing. We decide what we want to feel. Therefore, I want you to think about all of us. About Sara, about Nisha, about Subah, about me. But most importantly, about yourself.'

She paused, and Akash once again looked at his mother. Her face was calm now, as if she had faced her karma and now it was his turn.

The doorbell rang, and the sound accentuated the stillness.

Akash raised his hand when he saw his mother stir. 'I'll get it, Mom.'

He walked across the living room and opened the door.

'Hello, Akash. How are you doing today?' It was Mr Raichand.

'I'm okay. Please come in, sir.' Akash turned and went back inside. Raichand followed him, sat down on a single sofa and nodded to Akash's mother.

'Good afternoon, Laxmiji.'

'Good afternoon, Raichandji. Thanks for coming.'

Akash looked at both of them. Something was brewing. He decided to wait.

'Akash, I was the one who called Mr Raichand. I'm sorry I did so without asking you. Since you respect him so much, I thought you would like to hear his opinion too.'

'Ma...' Akash felt mild irritation, and it showed in the way he said 'Ma'. But perhaps his mother was right. There was no harm in it. It would be over in a few minutes, he was sure. Also, it was really a pleasure to see his boss again, someone he really trusted, admired and loved.

'Akash, I don't have to say anything. This is your business. But if you want to know my opinion, I'll be happy to share it with you.'

'Sir, I have always valued your opinion.'

'I know, thanks. Well, I think you feel trapped between a beautiful past that you can't let go of and a future that holds beautiful promise as well. Your fear is that the future will dominate the past. That it will take you away from Nisha and the world you shared with her. To be frank, anyone in your position would think that way.'

He paused, and Akash's mother was instantly on her feet, seizing the moment. 'Would you like some tea?'

He turned to look at her. 'Later, maybe. I want you to hear what I have to say as well.'

'Don't worry, I'll be able to hear you from the kitchen.'

He nodded, and she moved to the kitchen.

'Shall I continue?'

Akash nodded this time.

'So, the future… Yes, the future will eventually become the present and finally the past. Everything must eventually become the past. That's the rule of nature, and it can't be changed. Me, your mother, you, everything. But first, we have to live in the present. We have to inhabit it. If we do it happily, as you did with Nisha, we will have a happy past to lean on. In short, when we make our present happy, our existence has new meaning. Those who live in the present are the happiest. They make the best memories. They live, rather than just existing. You have to think about your present, Akash. You have to think about how you can find happiness for yourself and Sara. Because nothing can bring Nisha back, no matter what we do. The question is, can Subah be part of your present? Don't look to me for an answer. Don't think about what your mother said. Ask yourself. Face yourself.'

Akash's mother appeared with a tray containing three cups

of tea and a small plate of cookies. 'Tea for all of us.' She put the tray down, picked up the plate of cookies and extended it to Mr Raichand. 'And here, you must try these, Raichandji. They are my Akash's favourite cookies.'

But Akash was on his feet. 'Ma, I need some fresh air.'

They looked at each other.

His mother smiled and said, 'Of course you do, my son.'

Akash picked up his car keys, opened the door and walked out. When he heard the click of the door behind him, he knew he was finally alone. He exhaled loudly.

Chapter 54

Outside, the afternoon was warm, and before the air conditioner in his car could dissipate the heat, he was sweating. Was it really the heat or was it the pressure of the moment?

Did he know where he had to go?

The answer was *no*.

Did he know his decision?

The answer was *no*.

Would he be able to decide it now?

The answer was *yes*.

He got lost in a maze of thoughts as he drove. But he was not thinking about anything in particular. He was just floating in his mind. A little later, he found himself in the parking lot of the hospital where Nisha had breathed her last.

Why was he here?

He got out of the car and walked across to the reception area, as if he was being pulled in that direction. Five minutes later, he was talking to the nurse, Angel, who had taken care of his wife in her final days. She had recognized him and smiled, and they walked to the hospital café and sat at a table.

'How are you, Angel?'

'I'm fine. How are you holding up, sir? How is little Sara?' The nurse remembered Akash's daughter's name. He was touched.

'She's fine. I just thought I should thank you once more for everything you did during my wife's final days.'

'You're welcome. I remember her often, sir. She talked so much about you when she was here. Every nurse in the ICU secretly wished they had someone in their lives who loved them so dearly. Whenever she spoke about you or Sara, she would smile. No matter what kind of pain she was in, not only her face but her soul would light up. It's like you two had a connection that couldn't be broken by anything…' She looked away, as if searching for the right words, and continued after some time, 'You know what, I almost believed that her will to live her life with you and Sara would defeat cancer. All of us believed it. I prayed at the church. Her passing came as a crushing shock. Death may have silenced her soul, sir, but I know death can't kill the love she felt. I can feel it still, hanging in the air whenever I look at the bed she was in. I know time will dilute my memory of her, but I also know her love for you and Sara will live forever.'

With that, she stood up, reached for her purse and turned towards the door.

'Thank you' was all he could say.

She didn't turn, but Akash saw her nod. He was sure there were tears in her eyes. His were full of tears too.

After she'd gone, he put his head on the table in the café and slept. When he woke up, it was to someone lightly shaking his shoulder. He straightened and found himself staring at Angel. She held a tray with two steaming cups on it.

'Tea, sir.'

'Nisha was right in her letter. You're one of the kindest people I've ever met. Thank you.'

They had tea in silence, and after that, it was time for Akash to bid farewell to the nurse and the hospital. Even though he was emotionally exhausted, he felt lighter as he walked to his car.

He recalled what Nisha had written in her final letter:

Sooner or later, someone will get close to you again. Please allow it to happen. Don't ruin your life thinking about me. When you find someone, I want you to fall in love again. Think of that woman as me, and you can be happy again. I want you to be happy, I want Sara to have a family, and I want to be forgotten. I want you to merge us with your new life and start again.

Chapter 55

*A*s Akash drove, nothing came to his mind. It was as if someone had wiped his short-term memory clean. And then he remembered what his mother and Mr Raichand had said.

He turned his car into the parking lot of the Lodhi Gardens, switched off the engine, got out and slammed the door. In the distance, he could hear ducks bathing.

Akash walked through the wrought iron gates, over the footbridge, and looked to his right at the ducks in the water. He continued to walk until he found an empty bench and sat down. His head was spinning. He felt like a man jailed in a cell of his own thoughts. There seemed to be no way out.

He considered the equation with Subah. In many ways, he thought she was like him. She'd never come looking for him, just like he hadn't gone looking for her. His accidentally stepping into her exhibition, her sending a query within minutes of the launch of his online company, her being kidnapped in Mumbai, his visiting Mumbai, their getting close, none of that could have been planned. Those events were as natural as the movements of the earth and moon.

Was this the woman Nisha thought would get close to him, the one whose nearness she wanted him to allow to happen?

Connecting Nisha's letter to Subah kindled a fresh perspective in him. Two questions popped into his mind as he stretched his body on the bench. He lifted his face to the sky and closed his eyes, just as Nisha had asked him to. *Now close your eyes, Akash.* He had read those words so many times in her letter.

Did he like Subah? He did.

But did he love her? He indeed did, and yet, he needed time to contemplate the contours of their relationship.

One thing was clear. Their love wasn't something that had happened at first sight. It had built over time, first as they had swung away from each other, and then as various small and indiscernible events had brought them closer. Who was doing this? Was it someone other than the two of them? Was it some kind of divine power?

A parrot landed near his feet. Akash looked at the bird, and for a moment, thought his black eyes met the bird's grey. The parrot was just a foot from his shoes, and the first thing he noticed was its colour. He had never seen a parrot that was red and purple before. He moved his legs to startle it into leaving him alone with the biggest dilemma of his life, but the parrot didn't budge.

He decided to ignore it, and his thoughts turned to Nisha. Was it Nisha who wanted him to get close to Subah? Silly though this train of thought appeared, it could very well be her. He thought about her letter once more.

Akash closed his eyes and tried to imagine Nisha next to him. He felt a tug at his laces and opened his eyes. The parrot was pulling at the laces of his shoe. An idea struck him. However outlandish it was, what if his hunch was right and this bird was in some way connected to Nisha? There was only one way to check.

'I've fallen in love with Subah, and I want to marry her.' He was happy to at last be able to say what he'd wanted to.

The bird stirred and flew away. Was that an approval?

Later, when he would talk about the colourful parrot to others, someone would say that it had to be from the eclectus species, in which the females were more colourful than usual. But, the person would add, a frown on his face, no one had seen them in India, as the species was native to the islands near Australia.

Akash closed his eyes again and only opened them when it started to rain. He recalled what Nisha used to say: *We close our eyes in the shower but never in the rain.*

Was Nisha trying to communicate with him through the parrot and the rain? Yes, she had to be.

'Thank you, Nisha,' he murmured.

The rain soaked through his clothes and shoes, and he felt a chill as the wind started to blow after the rain stopped.

As he walked back to his car an hour later, he found himself thinking more about Subah. What did she think of him? She had never said that she loved him. But neither had he said the words. Would she say yes if he proposed? Would she be a good mother to Sara?

Even though his future was filled with uncertainty, he now knew that the boat of his life was no longer rudderless.

Chapter 56

Two days later, wearing his best suit, Akash was on his way to Zeros in Khan Market. Finally, everything had fallen into place. He'd had to work really hard, but he was able to plan everything in time. When he entered Zeros, a waiter escorted him to the table, where a bucket of champagne was waiting. The tablecloth was crisp and fresh. There were roses and orchids on the table, and alongside it, candelabra with flickering, fragrant candles. The music was just as he had instructed.

Akash had picked out the flowers at the florist he used to frequent when Nisha was alive. The shop was called The Flower Solution.

'Flowers can solve any problem,' the florist, a Bengali man of around thirty, always said. Over the years, he had helped Akash understand the significance of different flowers. Roses were for love. Yellow flowers for wishing someone would get well soon. And orchids—which he pronounced 'arcade'—for fertility. Lilies were best for funerals. He was a man who cared about what he sold, and Akash liked his enthusiasm and didn't mind listening to his recommendations.

Earlier today, as Akash had stood at the florist's after a year-long hiatus, his eyes were on the roses.

'Sir, red roses are the best.'

'Do you know why I need them?'

'Yes, Akash babu. A florist is a doctor of emotions. I can spot a buyer's mood from a mile away.'

Akash didn't know how to react.

'Go ahead, take these red roses. They will complement the love she feels for you.'

'Do you think I'm in love?'

'Yes, Akash babu, you are a man in love. I have no doubt.'

Back at the restaurant, Akash's thoughts were broken by a call from Rohit, who said he would be there in five minutes.

But why was Subah taking so long?

He looked at his watch. It was 7 in the evening.

Just then, he saw her walk towards him. Her eyes met his, and she smiled. She looked stunning in the simple salwar kameez she wore. He had never seen a more beautiful woman in his life. She was elegant, talented, someone who didn't fear speaking her mind. It was a combination that God created probably once in a hundred years.

Subah came and stopped near him. He stepped close and kissed her cheek before asking her to sit down. The waiter eased the chair in as she sat.

'What is all this, Akash?'

'Well, it's a surprise party.'

'But a surprise for whom and what's the occasion?'

'You'll see.' Akash winked.

Subah was confused. Akash had called her two days ago to invite her to this dinner. He'd said he wanted to discuss an important matter. Even though she had no idea what he wanted to discuss, she had said *yes* as a friend and a client. Since returning from Mumbai, she'd gotten his hint that he didn't want a repeat of what had happened there, and she'd reconciled herself to it. No matter what, Mumbai would be etched in her heart and mind forever.

She saw Rohit walking towards them and wondered what he was doing there.

'Hi, Subah. You look lovely.'

Rohit hugged Akash without waiting for her reply, and when they disengaged, he put his hand in his pocket and pulled out a small box. Akash took it from him and pocketed it. Rohit stepped back and stood a little distance from them.

What is in that box? Subah wondered.

Then she saw Akash bend one of his knees and rest it on the carpeted floor. As he got down on one knee, she thought to herself: *Oh my god, this can't be happening*!

She was still seated, and her mind had stopped working. She knew what came next, and yet she was not able to fully comprehend it.

'Will you marry me, Subah?'

She stood up, and their eyes met.

Akash was unable to read her expression. She took a small step towards him. He tried to imagine her thoughts. Why was she taking so long? He opened his mouth to say something. He wanted to say, *It's pointless to deny it, Subah. Say yes. Let's tie our paths together from this moment on. Let's give new meaning to the dream we saw in Mumbai.*

But his mouth remained shut. He saw her bend down, and now her face was very close to his, barely inches away. Her eyes scanned his face for answers to questions he thought he knew. He could smell her faint perfume as his senses started to come alive. He wanted to kiss her. But not until she said *yes*.

Chapter 57

*A*s Subah looked at him, she felt like time had stopped. This was a million-second moment for her, and not only her future but someone else's depended on it. She had to say *yes* or *no*. Her decision would be final. She held the key to their combined world. Was this moment a burden or a celebration?

What if she said *no*?

Everyone would accept it, of course. But what about Akash? He would accept it too, even though it would break his heart. That much she knew.

And what if she said *yes*?

It would bring joy to everyone she knew. Most importantly to Akash and Sara.

But what about her? Did she really want this? Perhaps she needed to think some more. Subah looked at the man before her. He was sincere, and his expression showed that he meant it.

What guaranteed that this man would not become like her father?

Would he trust her with his daughter?

What about his first wife, Nisha? Would Subah be able to make her own place in his heart?

Wasn't he lucky to put the question on her? Weren't men always lucky when it came to life's most difficult decisions? Like this? Or having a child? Or buying a house? Men controlled the lives that women led, making them choose what the men knew they would.

Subah wasn't able to decide what the best course of action was. Time stood still, as if her thoughts had frozen it.

'No.'

Did she really say that? Yes, of course she did. Some part of her, the rebellious part that she'd never tried to control, had said it. It was the practical part. Her brain.

But did she really mean to say *no*?

Was *no* her real answer to 'will you marry me, Subah'?

Subah placed her hand on her chest and tried to feel her heartbeat. Her heart was racing, but to where and for what? The decision had been made by her mind, the part that controlled her, the part that had seen what her dad did to her mother, the part that had bailed her out when the man she was in love with killed her trust.

And yet she wondered what her heart really wanted.

Subah closed her eyes. She wanted to shut everything out and see if she could make sense of her heart's rhythm. She immersed herself within herself, like a diver in search of a pearl.

Her heart was saying *yes*.

She opened her eyes. It was clear to her now. Her heart and mind were pulling her soul in different directions.

And then the puzzle started to unravel. *She* was the heart, and her *inner voice* was her mind.

It was a fight between what was natural and what was practical. Now was the time to take control.

What is your dream, Subah? she asked herself.

She'd always wanted to be a woman who was fearless and

independent, someone who used her mind but finally decided on what her heart desired. A woman who chose what she believed was best for her. A woman with a happy future. A woman with the power to nurture and make this world beautiful, caring and tolerant.

She spoke again: 'No, no matter what happens to me now, we will triumph over everything together, Akash. *Yes*, I will marry you.'

Akash took the hand that she extended, tugged it gently towards him, and brought it close to his mouth. He looked down at her hand and paused.

She could feel his breath on her hand. Akash's face broke into a smile. She had always loved his smile, but this one was special. Happiness transformed his face, and he looked exactly like the visions of him she'd been seeing these past few weeks.

Subah had met her destiny. Or perhaps Akash had met his. Better still, both had met theirs.

He kissed her hand, and they heard a loud cheer. Later, Akash would tell her how everyone had been watching him propose on a television screen in the next room. For now, all she knew was that their close family members and friends were present.

It was tough, but Akash had convinced Subah's mother to visit Delhi. He couldn't give her the real reason, as Subah had yet to say *yes*, so he had arranged for his mother and Subah's to have a word. That had worked, and she was there. Subah's father had stayed in the US, saying he was too busy. Akash's mother, Rohit, Mr Raichand, James, Lucky, Bala and little Sara were present too. Akash had sent a plane ticket to Mr Taraporewala, who was kind enough to come from Mumbai. And from Subah's

Jor Bagh office were Mr Samir Subramanian, Prerna and Aparna.

'Dad.' From amidst the loud cheering and clapping, Sara's voice emerged, and when everyone present turned their attention to her, she giggled and said, 'Now you may kiss the bride.'

'Yeeeessssss!' everyone present shouted in unison.

'As you know, I never say *no* to my daughter,' declared Akash as he watched Subah blush.

Chapter 58

*S*ubah and Akash were married one month from the day he proposed to her. It was a simple but elegant affair.

Akash had allowed Subah to make all the important decisions regarding the venue, decorations, food and their clothes. He kept his focus on the guest list and prepared his apartment so that Subah would feel welcome when she arrived.

While they discussed the minutest of the details about their wedding, Akash gained a clearer understanding of Subah's likes and dislikes. As the day drew nearer, with the help of his mother, Akash made every possible change to the apartment. This was a difficult decision for him because on the one hand, he wanted to make Subah feel at home, but on the other, he didn't want Nisha's memory to be diluted in any way.

Subah said she was happy, and he believed her. Akash was equally happy that Subah had accepted him and Sara in her life. In many ways, he thought she was a nicer human being than him and thanked Nisha for making sure they got together.

On their first morning as man and wife, Akash answered a knock at the door and was pleasantly surprised to see Mr Raichand. Subah was still asleep in the bedroom, and so were his mother and Sara in the other bedroom. The time was 7 in the morning, and the music from last night was still ringing in his ears.

'Good morning, Akash. May I come in?'

'Good morning, sir. Yes, please. I hope all is well.'

'Yes. Couldn't be better.'

They walked in and sat down in the living room.

Raichand smiled, and Akash wondered what his ex-boss was up to.

'Can I get you a cup of tea, sir?'

'No, thank you, Akash. The wonderful dinner at your wedding last night is still sitting here.' He patted his stomach before continuing. 'Congratulations once again. Where's Subah?'

Akash looked towards the bedroom door, and Raichand nodded, understanding. 'I would like to speak to both of you.'

'Sure, sir. You mean now?'

'Is that a problem?'

'No, sir.'

Akash went into the bedroom. At the same time, Akash's mother emerged from the other bedroom. 'Good morning, Raichandji.'

He was on his feet. 'Good morning, Laxmiji. I know it is early, but I won't take longer than five minutes, I promise.'

Ten minutes later, when Akash, Subah and Laxmi were sitting in the living room, Raichand began to speak. 'Akash and Subah, once again, congratulations on your wedding. I can't tell you how happy I am for both of you. Congratulations to you as well, Laxmiji. Now, to the real reason I'm here...'

He paused and looked at their faces one by one. The suspense was building, and no one had any clue why he was there so early right after the wedding. Raichand knew what was going through their minds, and he wanted it like that.

'Akash, I've seen the valuation of Johnnie Sparks, your

digital media company. It's valued at ₹2 crore. I want to buy a 50 per cent stake in it.' The other three looked at each other. 'In short, I want to give you ₹1 crore for making me an equal partner in your new firm.'

Akash's mouth opened, but no words came out. He couldn't believe what he'd just heard. His boss, someone he admired and hoped to be associated with for life, was asking him for a partnership. He wasn't sure if the valuation was right or if Mr Raichand had inflated it himself. Whatever the reason, this was an offer no one could refuse. He got up, and seeing him do so, the others got up too.

'Deal.'

Everyone cheered, and that brought Sara out, rubbing her eyes with one hand, the other dragging her soft toy, Wriggly the caterpillar.

'Dad, I'm hungry. Can we eat pizza, please?'

Epilogue

*A*kash drove down to the hospital as soon as Raichand had left. He moved through the people crowding the main foyer and entered the cafeteria.

It was time to respond to the storm that had been raging in his heart for many days now. It was time for closure.

He ordered a coffee and sat down to do what he had come there for. From his pocket, he pulled out Nisha's letter and placed his fingers on the words, his eyes closed as he imagined her writing it. After some time, he opened his eyes and read the letter one last time.

Finally, he turned it over and began to write on the other side, the side that was blank. It was now his turn to communicate.

My dearest Nisha,

This letter is long overdue.

When you were here with me and Sara, I thought I was the luckiest man on the planet. I've never loved anyone or anything more dearly than I loved you. And after you were gone, I thought I was the unluckiest man. That is what your presence meant to me.

During the last year, ever since you left us, I've thought of you every day. I know you are no longer here with us, but the memory of what we shared is so vivid that I've always sensed your presence next to me and Sara.

Yes, I'd said that letters have permanence. And that is why I'm writing this final letter to you. Even though the disease snatched you from us, your thoughts in your letter guided me at every step.

Sara is just like you. Every time she looks at me, I think you're trying to communicate with me. Is that an illusion, or are you really watching us through her eyes? I know you can't answer, just as I know that as long as I'm close to Sara, I'll always be close to you.

You made our life beautiful, Nisha. You did small but important things in the house, and it was because of your love that I could excel in the office. With you by my side, I was healthier, happier and more focused. When I found you, I discovered a new kind of gravity. And therefore, no matter how far away you are now, my thoughts will always keep you close to me.

Do you remember when we got drenched in the rain at Sarojini Nagar? That day, you taught me how to appreciate the small things in life. That happiness and calm are not outside us but within us. My understanding of life was shaped by you, my love, and now I'm doing all that I can to make sure that our Sara grows into a beautiful and talented human being, just like you.

I miss you so terribly some days, Nisha, that I wonder if I would be better off dead. At least in death, I would be closer to you.

But now, I've decided to move on, as you asked me to do. Subah is wonderful. In many ways, she's like you. I ask myself how that can be possible and then I'm reminded of your letter. Without my anticipating it, the world we made and the future that awaits me are about to merge with each other. Only you could have seen this before I did. Today is the first day of us together as a family. I know we will be fragile in the beginning, but I promise that I will work hard to make it work.

As you directed, I presented your bangles to Angel. The other day, when I was feeling weak and missing you terribly, she bought me a cup of tea. You were right—she indeed has a heart of gold.

Ma misses you a lot too. She doesn't say it, but I can tell.

Thank you for being such a wonderful lover, a great mother and an amazing friend. When I'm finally among the stars, I'll be looking out for you too. It will be easy for me, won't it? I know you will be shining the brightest. I'll just have to turn towards the brightest star and keep moving until I reach you.

With all my love for you,

Your lucky husband,

Akash